Career Mastery Unleashed: Your Blueprint for Success, And Proven Strategies for Climbing the Career Ladder

By

Jose R. Johnson

1

Disclaimer
The data gave on this stage is to general enlightening inspirations as it were. While I endeavor to stay up with the latest and exact, Jose R. Johnson makes no portrayals or guarantees of any sort, express or suggested, about the culmination, precision, dependability, appropriateness, or accessibility concerning the substance or the data, items, benefits, or related designs contained on this stage for any reason. Any dependence you put on such data is thusly stringently notwithstanding all advice to the contrary.

In no occasion will Jose R. Johnson be obligated for any misfortune or harm, including without limit, backhanded or considerable misfortune or harm, or any misfortune or harm at all emerging from loss of information or benefits emerging out of, or regarding, the utilization of this stage.Through this stage, you can connection to different sites that are not heavily influenced by Jose R. Johnson. I have no control over the nature, content, or accessibility of those locations. The consideration of any connections doesn't be guaranteed to suggest a proposal or support the perspectives communicated inside here.

Each work is made to flawlessly keep the stage ready. In any case, Jose R. Johnson assumes a sense of ownership with, and won't be obligated for, the stage being briefly inaccessible because of specialized issues unchangeable as far as I might be concerned.

Table of contents:

INTRODUCTION

Setting the Stage for Career Excellence

Your career is the main act in the grand theater of life, where hopes, dreams, and aspirations are realized. You walk into the spotlight every day prepared to perform, adjust, and grow. Your career is a canvas on which you paint the masterpiece of your professional life, not just a way to make ends meet. Welcome to "Building an Elite Career," a manual that will enable you to write the success story of your own.

This book is your backstage pass to the elite world of professional achievement, where the commonplace becomes extraordinary. You'll find all the tips, tricks, and motivation you need in these pages to lay the groundwork for a genuinely outstanding career.

Imagine being able to confidently and clearly define your professional path, transforming your identity into a strong brand that appeals to others. Imagine becoming an expert in time management, bringing order to chaos, and increasing your output. Imagine the excitement of successfully establishing meaningful connections, perfecting your communication techniques, and networking.

"Building an Elite Career" is a journey rather than just a manual. It serves as your individual mentor, coach, and encouragement as you pursue greatness. This book will provide you with the skills, knowledge, and inspiration to pave the way for your own professional success, regardless of whether you're a recent graduate looking to make your professional debut, a mid-career professional looking for fresh challenges, or an experienced professional striving for the highest level of achievement.

As we set out on this life-changing adventure, keep in mind that achieving success in an elite career isn't the only goal. It's about accepting the never-ending path of development, learning, and self-improvement. Similar to a well-rehearsed performance, your career requires commitment, practice, and an openness to change. Now that the stage is set and the spotlight is on you, take a front row seat. Starting today, you can embark on an exceptional career path.

What it takes to build an elite career

Like a major performance, your career is an ongoing act that calls for skill, commitment, and a never-ending quest of perfection. Achieving the highest level of success isn't the only thing that goes into creating an elite career; you also need to embrace the process, keep improving, and develop into the best version of yourself in the workplace. We will reveal the essential components that are essential to pursuing a top career in this comprehensive guide. These tips will assist you in laying the foundation for your own professional success, regardless of where you are in your career or your goals for it.

1. Clarity and Vision
Any great career starts with a well-defined vision. What goals do you have in mind? Where

do you see yourself in five, ten, or twenty years? Having a clear career vision that acts as your compass is imperative. You can make a road map that shows the steps you need to take to get there if you have a clear destination in mind.

2. Establishing Objectives

You need to break down your vision into attainable objectives. These goals must be SMART, which stands for specified, measurable, achievable, relevant, and time-bound. You provide yourself with distinct benchmarks to aim for when you establish clear, attainable goals. Establishing goals helps you track your progress and maintains motivation.

3. Education for Life

Maintaining current knowledge is crucial in the ever evolving field of professional work. Make learning your lifelong goal. Participate in workshops, read books, watch industry trends on the internet, and take online courses. In addition to keeping your skills current, being a lifelong learner shows that you are dedicated to your own development.

4. Flexibility

The only thing that is constant in today's workplace is change. It's critical to have the flexibility to adjust to new tasks, workflows, and technologies. The foundation of an outstanding career is adaptability and a readiness to accept change. Adaptability is key to staying relevant and valuable in your field.

5. Sturdiness

Challenges and disappointments are common in the path of an elite career. The capacity to overcome hardship and preserve your will and motivation is known as resilience. When you encounter challenges, see them as chances for personal development and keep going.

6. Establishing Networks and Relationships

One's network can be just as valuable in the workplace as one's knowledge. It's critical to establish a strong network and cultivate relationships within your industry. Participate in conferences, join groups for professionals, and establish a routine of reaching out to mentors and colleagues.

7. Building Oneself

Creating a strong personal brand is essential in today's competitive employment market. Your personal brand is how other people see you and your values. Create an authentic, recognizable, and clear personal brand that supports your professional objectives.

8. Skillful Interaction

In an elite career, effective communication skills are essential. Your capacity for persuasive and clear communication is a critical component of your success in the workplace, whether you're negotiating, resolving conflicts, or expressing your ideas.

9. Organizing Your Time

Since time is a limited resource, the way you use it can have a big influence on your career.

Proficient individuals possess exceptional time management skills, effectively plan their workday, and prioritize tasks to optimize productivity.

10. Teamwork and Leadership

Managers are not the only ones who can exercise leadership. Knowing how to encourage, collaborate, and inspire others is essential whether you're the team leader or just one of the team members. Elite workers are adept at both teamwork and leadership.

11. Prudent Management

A skill that is applicable outside of one's personal life is financial literacy. Effective money management, from investing to budgeting, can provide you financial peace of mind and the freedom to make choices that advance your career.

12. Equilibrium Work-Life

It's critical for your long-term professional success as well as your well-being to maintain a healthy work-life balance. A base of well-being is the foundation of an elite career. Being in good physical and mental health makes you more capable of performing at your best.

13. Ability to Solve Problems

An elite career requires problem-solving on a daily basis. Experts in their fields are skilled at recognizing problems, evaluating information, and developing original solutions.

14. Honoring Inclusion and Diversity

Prominent professionals understand the value of inclusiveness and diversity in the workplace. By fostering an atmosphere where everyone feels appreciated and included, they help the company become more inventive and successful.

15. Mentoring and Contributing

Elite careers are defined by mentoring and giving back to the community or industry. Not only does sharing your expertise and experiences benefit others, but it also supports your own learning and development.

16. Continuous Self-Development

An elite career is a process rather than a final goal. It necessitates continuous personal development. Set new objectives, evaluate your abilities on a regular basis, and push yourself to improve from yesterday.

17. Adopting Digital

It is imperative to embrace technology in the digital age. Technology is essential to developing a successful career, whether it is for understanding data analytics, staying up to date with the newest software, or making the most of social media.

18. Honesty and Morality

It is critical to uphold a high standard of integrity and moral behavior. In the business sector, trust is a valuable resource. Maintaining moral principles in everything you do is necessary for a fruitful and long-lasting career.

19. Accepting Input

Feedback is a very useful tool for development. Proficient individuals embrace critical criticism, apply it to their work, and never stop improving.

20. Creating the Conditions for Greatness

Developing a stellar career is an ongoing process. Dedication, self-awareness, and a commitment to progress are necessary for the journey. You'll be well on your way to building a career that not only fulfills but surpasses your highest hopes if you have these essential components in place. Now, let's examine each of these elements in more detail and learn the precise steps you can take to create the conditions for your own professional success.

Developing an elite career requires self-awareness, development, and adaptability. You can create the conditions for your own professional success by having a clear vision, committing to lifelong learning, and developing professionally and personally. You have to travel the road ahead with grit and excitement, as it is

full   of   opportunities,   obstacles,   and
accomplishments.

CHAPTER 1:

Your Career Blueprint

Regarding careers, there isn't a one-size-fits-all strategy. A person's solution may not work for another.

The most crucial thing is to figure out what you have to do to advance.

Do your skills need to be updated?

Make a fresh portfolio of your work?

Concentrate on your execution?

Establish a network?

or... anything like that?!?

Regardless of your professional stage, it's critical to regularly review and revise your roadmap for growth. You'll raise your chances of success and get one step closer to realizing your objectives if you do this.

Your Ideal Career Path: Consider

What then are a career blueprint's four sections?

You 1.

You are the first area. You must examine yourself honestly if you want to progress in your career. What are your advantages and disadvantages? Which life events have influenced the path of your career? What impressions do managers, coworkers, and other colleagues have of you? Understanding your personal brand starts with an honest self-evaluation of your professional self.

2. An Account

Your collection of work is your portfolio. The majority of people possess the necessary tools for advancing their careers, like a LinkedIn profile and resume. Still, think of your portfolio as a collection of your finest pieces. Excerpts from the projects you've only worked on are welcome, but more importantly, your portfolio should showcase your best work, such as an exceptionally well-executed idea or outcome. Making sure your portfolio is current and offers strong evidence to support the story you want to tell about your professional goals is crucial if you want to grow in your career.

3. Execution

For many, performance is directly related to job performance. Are you fulfilling or going above and beyond? Do you possess a solid history? Performance, however, also represents a mindset that prioritizes ongoing education, skill development, upskilling, and the ability to demonstrate a steady state of advancement. Making sure you're giving your best work and concentrating on your performance are crucial if you want to grow in your career.

It's crucial to remember, though, that performance also has to do with your capacity to share your narrative with people you want to impress. Both during an interview and when you're out and about networking with other professionals, you need to be prepared to sell yourself.

Do you feel at ease providing samples of your work that demonstrate why someone should hire you? Many job seekers are aware of what makes them stand out from the competition, and they will often cite accomplishments or examples from their resume. To really put your storytelling abilities to use, though, you should practice pitching to potential employers by becoming more comfortable and convincing when relating your experiences.

4. Humans

Finally, the individuals you associate with in your professional life can have a significant influence on the course of your career. Even though a lot of job searchers rapidly enlist the help of coworkers and other people who can recommend them for a future opportunity, your network should represent a variety of viewpoints. Think about creating your own Personal Board of Advisors by reaching out to new people in your network. The important voices on this board should serve as your guides as you pursue your career.

Key roles could be, for instance:

. A mentor is a person who can offer guidance or understanding; they are usually highly acquainted with the necessary steps to achieve the desired outcome.

. A role model is someone who embodies the values and goals you have.

. A connector, or the person who serves as the "hub" of relationships and is constantly aware of new roles or opportunities, and a

The sponsor. Sponsors play a crucial role in your career development because they are powerful individuals who can help you grow and often extend invitations to take advantage of opportunities that are not readily available to most professionals.

. Building a strong network of people you can trust, who can support and assist you, and who share your views is essential if you want to progress in your career.

These four areas are crucial for career advancement no matter where you are in your career.

Defining Your Path to Success

Achievement is a word that is in many cases tossed around in our day to day discussions. Whether it's working, in our own lives, or in the media, we are continually barraged with messages about what achievement ought to resemble. Be that as it may, what does achievement truly mean? Also, for what reason is it alright not to contrast ourselves with others' lives?

As per the word reference, achievement is "the achievement of a point or reason." This definition suggests that achievement is private and emotional. What may be viewed as fruitful for one individual may not be for another. For some purposes, achievement could mean accomplishing monetary dependability, while for other people; it could mean having a satisfying vocation or a blissful day to day life.

Over the course of the past many years, the meaning of progress has developed. Achievement, first and foremost, was in many cases characterized by material belongings and monetary riches. Individuals sought to possess enormous homes, extravagant vehicles, and costly garments. In any case, as society advanced, individuals began to understand that material belongings weren't guaranteed to be like joy or achievement. Over the most recent 20 years the meaning of achievement moved towards individual satisfaction and self-realization. Individuals started to focus on their own joy and prosperity over cultural assumptions. This prompted an emphasis on taking care of oneself, care, and self-awareness.

Today, achievement is more nuanced than any time in recent memory. It incorporates a large number of variables, including monetary soundness, vocation fulfillment, self-awareness, and social effect. The best individuals are the people who can adjust these various parts of their lives and track down satisfaction in all areas.

Achievement comes in many structures, and it's vital to commend every one of them, since that assists us with perceiving our own accomplishments, regardless of how enormous or little, and it urges us to keep on endeavoring towards our objectives. It likewise assists us with valuing the one of a kind ways that others are on and perceive their achievements as well.

Tracking down your own meaning of accomplishment

The initial step is to characterize how achievement affects you. Carve out an opportunity to think about what is really essential to you and what you need to accomplish in your life. This could include defining explicit objectives, like beginning a business, composing a book, or venturing to the far corners of the planet. It could likewise include more unique ideas, like self-improvement, satisfaction, and satisfaction. When you have a reasonable thought of how achievement affects you, make an arrangement to accomplish your objectives. Finding your own rendition of accomplishment might require acquiring new abilities, organizing with similar individuals, and facing challenges outside your usual range of familiarity. Recall that achievement is certainly not a direct interaction, and there will be promising and less promising times en route. Remain on track, remain roused, and remain consistent with yourself, and you will track down your own form of progress.

Anyway, for what reason is it OK not to contrast ourselves with others' lives?

First and foremost, on the grounds that everybody's process is unique. We as a whole have our own one of a kind situation, difficulties, and objectives. Contrasting ourselves with others is a recipe for dissatisfaction and disappointment.

Besides, examination is a cheat of delight. At the point when we center a lot around what others have, we neglect to focus on what we have achieved and the headway we have made. Rather than contrasting ourselves with others, we ought to zero in on our own advancement and commend our own triumphs, regardless of how little they might appear.

Ultimately, be somewhat childish with your prosperity, since when we are narrow minded with progress, we are bound to accomplish our objectives and track down satisfaction in our lives. By zeroing in on our own excursion, we can gain ground towards our own meaning of accomplishment, as opposed to attempting to satisfy another person's assumptions. This permits us to construct self-assurance, versatility, and a feeling of direction.

Achievement is an individual and emotional idea that has developed over the long run. Instead of contrasting ourselves with others, we ought to zero in on our own excursion and praise our own achievements. Achievement isn't an objective; an excursion requires difficult work, devotion, and constancy. With the right outlook and a promise to self-awareness, anybody can make their variant of progress.

CHAPTER 2:

Crafting Your Professional Image

Laying out areas of strength for a picture assists people with keeping up with positive working environment connections and presenting themselves properly. Being aware of how you dress, talk and act around others is significant while satisfying your everyday obligations or while attempting to progress into another job. Looking further into what an expert picture is and understanding the moves toward foster it can assist you with introducing yourself reliably working..

In this article, I characterize what an expert picture is, recognize its parts and give 10 supportive tips to assist you with fostering your expert picture.

What is an expert picture?

An expert picture depicts the manner in which an individual behaves at work and in other expert settings. It additionally includes the demeanor they use at work and how others see them. Individuals frequently take a stab at an expert picture that lines up with the assumptions for their specific working environment or industry, as it can assist people with impacting choices and structure significant business associations. It can likewise assist individuals with speaking with others all the more actually.

Parts of an expert picture

Your expert picture comprises four key parts. Understanding these parts and their job in your expert picture can help you while making any appraisals about how you introduce yourself at work. These four parts are:

- **Correspondence style:** Your discussion propensities and the language you pick are both piece of your expert picture. This alludes to how you talk about yourself, others and your work and the tone and words you use.

- **Conduct and mentality:** Your outlook towards your work can adversely affect your efficiency, and others can frequently detect your disposition in view of your ways of behaving. Stepping up to the plate, tending to liability and empowering others are ways of behaving that mirror an expert disposition.

- **Nonverbal correspondence:** Nonverbal correspondence might incorporate your stance, eye to eye connection and hand signals, all of which can convey your considerations and feelings in manners by which you may not be cognizant, yet which can in any case influence how others see you.

- **Clothing and preparing:** How you dress and style yourself for work and other expert social affairs influences your expert picture. Exhibiting regard for your appearance reflects certainty and gives

others the feeling that you figure out your social job in the work environment.
Instructions to foster your expert picture

The following are 10 ways to make a positive expert picture:

1. Be aware of initial feelings

Individuals structure initial feelings rapidly, and these impressions can affect situations like new employee screenings and gatherings with new clients. By being aware of your appearance and direct in these circumstances, you can project a more sure expert picture. The following are three components to consider while meeting another expert contact or entering what is happening that can assist with initial feelings:

- **Industry shows:** Consider which ways of behaving and characteristics are normal for an expert in a specific industry and how you like to carry them out in your own particular manner.

- **Working environment picture:** Ponder how others as of now see your situation at work and whether their impression lines up with your aims.

- **Ideal interest group:** This alludes to the various collaborations you have at a work environment, incorporating discussions with partners, bosses or clients.

2. Evaluate your correspondence style

To show amazing skill when you connect with others, you can utilize specific verbal and nonverbal methods. Consider utilizing an unmistakable discourse example to assist you with passing on your motivation and express precise data, which others might like if you work on an undertaking together. Contingent upon your solace level, it might very well be useful to support some eye to eye connection and screen the volume of your voice so you can all the more likely adjust your activities to the tone of a discussion. You can likewise rehearse undivided attention during discussions, meaning you stay connected with when somebody is talking and reflect data back to them.

You might profit from checking on your composed correspondence too. For instance, assuming others frequently pose explaining inquiries about any messages or messages you send, it might imply that your composed correspondence needs lucidity. Taking into account how others might decipher your message can assist you with distinguishing on the off chance that your composed correspondence needs significant data.

3. Consider what your garments reflect about you

While it's vital to dress inside your means, consider whether your ordinary clothing meets both composed and unwritten standards about apparel in your work environment.. Composed rules might be rules in a representative handbook, while unwritten principles might incorporate the size, variety or style of adornments and articulation pieces. You can get a feeling of unwritten principles by noticing your partners and taking note of similitudes in their dress styles. When you comprehend these rules, executing style decisions you appreciate can build your certainty, which might assist you with playing out your work liabilities effectively.

If conceivable, lessen the quantity of kinks in your dress and sew any tears you track down in the texture. Keeping your clothing slick broadens its life, and it shows that you care about your job and others' thought process of you.

4. Utilize online entertainment insightfully

Due to web-based entertainment's expanded presence, it's vital to be aware of the variant of yourself you present on the web. Regardless of whether your own records aren't openly visible, it's great practice to expect that others can in any case share and view anything you post via virtual entertainment. Accordingly, ponder how your posts do or don't match the expert picture you're developing working. By being reliable about your picture both in the work environment and on the web, you can stay away from any likely slips up about how others see your disposition and conduct.

5. Increment your time usage abilities

Stay dependable while going to gatherings, introductions or different occasions. Showing up on time can convey major areas of strength for an incredible skill, as it frequently recognizes your partners and their obligations. To build your possibilities beginning on time, it might be useful to set up your materials in advance. Think about utilizing an organizer or booking application to sort out occasions during a typical business day and record your commitments. To figure out how to advance your time, you can likewise set clocks to more readily comprehend what amount of time each undertaking requires.

6. Track down a guide

Find a partner or boss who can assist you with figuring out how to explore and keep up with proficient connections, which is a significant part of your expert picture. Consider choosing a couple of competitors and have a casual chance to figure out who may be an ideal coach for your character, inclinations and targets. In the wake of laying out a tutor relationship, it could be useful to set a sensible gathering plan and set up your requests ahead of time so you can have more valuable discussions.

7. Stay positive

Think about moving toward new circumstances in the work environment hopefully. Communicating a warm and sure expert picture in specific situations might be gainful. Another client or partner might see the value in a caring activity, as this kind of energy can assist somebody with feeling more good. For instance, you can have a go at hello individuals with energy and a consistent handshake. You can likewise urge individuals to move toward startling issues with a useful perspective, which can assist with creating a positive mentality and produce arrangements.

8. Be responsible

Take care of your activities to show you can circle back to other people. This shows trustworthiness and a longing to work on your lead, which might motivate others to show similar viewpoints in their own proficient pictures. In the event that a circumstance at any point has surprising outcomes, you can find an opportunity to consider your activities and techniques for tackling issues all the more effectively later on. Think about asking a partner for their own viewpoint on a circumstance, as this activity recognizes their experience and ability.

9. Reinforce your capacity to understand individuals on a profound level

The capacity to appreciate individuals on a deeper level includes the capacity to see the mind-sets of others and modify your way of behaving as needs be. To upgrade your expert picture, learning the needs and inspirations of others might be useful. Businesses and partners frequently value a person who can answer feelings beneficially, as they can all the more likely locate the necessities of an organization and put down supportive stopping points. For instance, on the off chance that a partner communicates worry about a work project, you can console them of their capacities and pose key inquiries so you both can define reachable objectives.

10. Go to systems administration occasions

Go to a systems administration occasion like a studio or workshop to foster more industry associations, which might assist you with keeping a positive standing. While meeting another companion, get familiar with their name and pose important inquiries about their life and work. It's likewise critical to talk certainly about your own work, as this activity can convey your ability and authoritative abilities. It could be useful to investigate the occasion in advance so you can pick an ideal attire style and get ready supportive conversational subjects.

After an occasion, it's smart to connect with any new contacts through email or expert web-based entertainment, contingent upon the data you traded. This shows that you esteem the association and are available to help them expertly assuming an open door emerges.

Building a Strong Personal Brand

In the present serious world, it is crucial for fabricate major areas of strength for a. Particularly for the people who need to separate themselves against others in their field and make a positive, dependable and powerful effect.
Be that as it may, what even is an individual brand? An individual brand can be characterized as a particular picture, notoriety and view of a person that they present to the world. The extended picture of a singular grandstands their character and mastery that characterizes their exceptional personality.

Having a strong individual brand set up permits individuals to see what your identity is, what you do and find out about your story. Gathering an individual brand is about deliberately dealing with the insights and relationship of yourself that people have of you both by and by and expertly.

Besides the fact that a very much created individual brand permits you to lay out believability yet in addition permits you to encounter new open doors, which is the reason we think constructing an individual brand is imperative. Continue pursuing to find the reason why individual marking is fundamental and the way that you can assemble your own.

The Advantages of an Individual Brand

Before we examine how to develop an individual brand, we really want to discuss why you really want one. Building an individual brand accompanies a few great advantages that are significant for your own and proficient development. Building an individual brand is an interest in yourself and your future, making you ready to progress.

A portion of the principal benefits include:

1. An individual brand separates you from the opposition: In the consistently cutthroat work market and world, you generally need to search for ways of separating yourself. This is especially significant for understudies who have little insight and need to stand apart from their kindred alumni. An individual brand permits you to share your extraordinary characteristics, abilities and skill, which will make you more significant.

2. An individual brand further develops perceivability: Having a laid out private brand works on your perceivability inside your specialty or industry. By expanding your perceivability you extend your chances, making it more straightforward for others to interface with you for potential work jobs, joint efforts or associations. A solid brand goes about as a magnet, attracting potential open doors that line up with your objectives as well as assist you with contacting them more straightforwardly.

3. An individual brand makes believability: In the functioning scene, validity and trust go far. At the point when you have great individual marking, you work on your believability and entrust with your crowd. At the point when you reliably convey important bits of knowledge and exhibit your skill, you're laying down a good foundation for yourself as a solid power inside your industry.

4. An individual brand improves systems administration and joint effort: Individual marking opens ways to energizing systems administration and cooperation potential open doors. Having a decent private brand permits you to interface with different experts, industry specialists and possible guides. These recently established associations can prompt things, for example, organizations and coordinated effort to assist with guiding your vocation in the correct bearing.

5. An individual brand prompts professional success: Individual marking will prompt professional success, whether that be in your ongoing work environment or your future job. Managers are drawn to those with a solid individual brand as it exhibits impressive skill and a history of progress. An individual brand likewise empowers nonstop learning and development which helps vocation movement.

Ways to construct an Individual Brand

Building an individual brand doesn't work out more or less by accident, it requires investment, exertion and a viable methodology. Presently you are familiar with the fantastic benefits of having an individual brand, you're most likely considering how you can construct one of your own. Here are a few hints:

1. Characterize your image personality: First, you want to begin by recognizing your image character and what separates you from others in your field. To do this, you want to initially recognize your qualities, encounters, abilities and interests. You want to feature the special viewpoint and ability you can offer your crowd. By having a center, you can shape how you're seen by others and what you're known for.

2. Make your expert story: To make areas of strength for a brand, you really want to foster a contending proficient story. At the point when you know what your identity is, what you need and what you can offer is fundamental while building your story. You really want to foster a story that features your expert process, accomplishments, difficulties and errors. Individuals recall stories, and on the off chance that you do it admirably, this is the thing most experts will recollect when they think about you.

3. Construct serious areas of strength for a presence: In the present innovation driven world, to make an individual brand, then, at that point, you want to ensure you're centered around building a web-based presence. We suggest building an expert site or portfolio that highlights your story, mastery and exhibits the entirety of your persistent effort. We likewise exhort utilizing online entertainment stages, for example, LinkedIn and making content that mirrors your skill as well as reverberates with your crowd. By sharing valuable substance, taking part in web-based networks and drawing in with different experts, you're effectively working on your perceivability inside your field.

4. Focus on systems administration: Building an individual brand implies that you want to effectively organize and team up with experts both on the web and disconnected. Make a point to go to occasions in your industry, partake in online classes, join discussions and take part in any space where you can make new expert associations. By taking part in these significant discussions, you're getting your name out there, acquiring openness to new crowds and growing your scope.

5. Be predictable: Consistency is key while building anything, particularly your own image.

If you have any desire to be known as somebody with the most recent understanding and information, then you really want to keep up with consistency in your own marking across all stages. Whether this is routinely refreshing your portfolio with the most recent work you've done or refreshing your online entertainment stages, you really want to remain steady to fabricate trust.

6. Track down a tutor: Guides are much of the time old pros who could go on and on about ascending the company pecking order and building an individual brand. They've been in the shoes of their mentee previously and can share their insight and understanding in view of their past encounters. Finding a tutor implies you have somebody to help and guide you in the correct bearing.

7. Look for criticism: Criticism is fundamental to see development in every aspect of development. By acquiring input from people around you, whether it's your tutor or your crowd, you're ready to acquire understanding into how your own image is seen. Pay attention to the input given and adjust on a case by case basis to guarantee that you're constantly attempting to improve and refine your own image.

Building a strong individual brand accompanies so many advantages that individuals can't stand to pass up in the serious work space. Keep in mind, fabricating an individual brand needn't bother with being overpowering and upsetting. By characterizing your image personality, making an expert story, fabricating a web-based presence, effectively organizing, remaining reliable, finding a coach and looking for criticism, you ought to have the option to construct serious areas of strength for an in the blink of an eye and set up a good foundation for yourself as a compelling figure in your field.

CHAPTER 3:

Time Management Mastery

Using time effectively includes arranging and controlling the time spent on unambiguous exercises to maintain a flexible mindset. It helps us focus on and be more effective. Accomplishing a sound balance between fun and serious activities, and that implies adjusting our work and individual life, is essential; time usage assumes a critical part in accomplishing this equilibrium. At the point when we are purposeful with our time, it becomes simpler to keep up with this equilibrium. Adjusting work and individual life can likewise further develop our psychological and profound prosperity.

Compelling using time effectively and balance between serious and fun activities benefit our expert life and generally speaking prosperity. Growing great time usage abilities takes time and practice, yet once dominated, they can assist us with monitoring our average business day while partaking in our own life. Balance between fun and serious activities brings positive advantages like diminished pressure and additional opportunity for family and friends and family. By dealing with our time successfully, we can further develop our work life, increment efficiency, lower pressure, and construct a positive balance between fun and serious activities.

This article gives important bits of knowledge and common sense ways to dominate using time productively and accomplishing a solid balance between fun and serious activities. All through the article, we investigate different parts of using time productively and balance between serious and fun activities, including grasping difficulties, laying out clear boundaries and objectives, really assigning time, laying out limits, appointing undertakings, utilizing efficient apparatuses and innovation, rehearsing taking care of oneself, and making the most of expert advancement valuable open doors.

By perusing this article, you can acquire a more profound comprehension of the significance of using time productively and balance between fun and serious activities, as well as down to earth procedures and methods for working on your efficiency, diminishing pressure, and accomplishing your objectives. Whether you need to further develop your time usage abilities, accomplish a better balance between serious and fun activities, or look into these fundamental subjects, this article has something for everybody.

Figuring out the Difficulties

Adjusting work and individual life can be testing, and a significant number of us battle to accomplish a sound balance between serious and fun activities. Normal difficulties incorporate unreasonable requests, absence of control, unsupportive connections, absence of assets, high-feelings of anxiety, and worldwide rivalry. Likewise, consistent interruptions from correspondence innovation, open-office floor plans, and our steady connectedness make finding a harmony among work and individual life troublesome.

Different difficulties might ininclud

- Consecutive gatherings that allow for different errands.

- The assumption to continuously be accessible for work.

- A pointless demeanor towards balance between fun and serious activities.

These difficulties can make it hard to oversee time really, focus on undertakings, and keep a good arrangement between work responsibilities and individual life.

Unfortunate using time effectively can adversely affect both individual and expert life. It can prompt diminished efficiency, missed cutoff times, and constant delay. Unfortunate using time effectively can likewise cause pressure, uneasiness, and lower confidence. In the long haul, it can adversely influence connections, satisfaction, and by and large wellbeing. Unfortunate using time productively can prompt burnout, a failure to disengage from work, and a diminished capacity to interface with others. At long last, unfortunate using time productively can bring about monetary misfortunes, negative working environment connections, and missed cutoff times. It can likewise block our capacity to properly adjust work and life.

Laying out Boundaries and Objectives

Laying out clear boundaries and objectives is fundamental for individual and expert turn of events. It assists us with zeroing in on the main thing, disposes of disarray, and drives us toward our ideal objective. Defining clear boundaries and objectives permits us to deal with our time better, increment inspiration, and make a suitable arrangement to accomplish our goals.

Objective setting triggers new ways of behaving, guides our concentration, advances an identity dominance, and supports energy throughout everyday life. It assists us with adjusting our concentration and can prompt huge achievement and execution. Defining objectives permits us to quantify our advancement, deal with our time and endeavors all the more actually, and further develop regions that need consideration.

We can follow a few hints and techniques to order undertakings and adjust needs to our qualities. One methodology is to make a rundown of undertakings and rank them by their degree of significance. This positioning assists us with figuring out which undertakings to focus on over others.

Another methodology is to utilize the ABCDE strategy, which includes relegating a letter worth to each errand as per its significance. 'A' undertakings are first concern, while 'E' errands are low need. This technique permits us to in like manner arrange our assignments and tackle them.

It is likewise vital to distribute time for each errand and utilize a timetable to coordinate our everyday needs. Plans assist us with better dealing with our time and guarantee we center around the most basic errands.

Adjusting needs to values includes figuring out our profound convictions and convictions at work and home. We can adjust needs to values by wondering why we do what we do and distinguishing the top qualities that drive our way of behaving. Thus, we can realign our own and proficient needs in a manner that rouses us to continue to push ahead.

Viable Time Distribution Systems

We can utilize a few time usage methods to dispense our time really and increment efficiency.

These methods include:

- Defining Savvy obobjectives

- Focusing on assignments in view of significance and time limits

- Enjoying reprieves

- Arranging ourselves

- Eliminating trivial errands

- Arranging

Different strategies incorporate utilizing the Pomodoro Strategy, which includes breaking work into stretches utilizing a clock, applying the Pareto standard (otherwise called the 80/20 rule), which expresses that 20% of activities are liable for 80% of results, and utilizing a schedule to plan errands and arrangements.

Breaking assignments into sensible lumps and staying away from stalling are fundamental methodologies for successful time portion. To break undertakings into reasonable pieces, we can isolate bigger ventures into more modest, more sensible errands. This approach assists us with beating overpowering sentiments and gaining ground in more modest advances.

To keep away from delaying, we can perceive when we are lingering, commit explicit time for assignments, set cutoff times, embrace defects, and prize ourselves for finishing jobs. Establishing a useful workplace by finding or making a space that assists us with centering is likewise fundamental.

By carrying out these methods, we can more readily deal with our time, increment efficiency, diminish pressure, and equilibrium work and individual life.

Limits and Appointment

Laying out limits and imparting really is pivotal for accomplishing a good overall arrangement among work and individual life. Limits are the cutoff points we set for us and convey to others through activity or correspondence. They assist us with characterizing what we really want to feel secure and amazing and make apparatuses to safeguard those pieces of ourselves.

Successful correspondence is basic for laying out limits. It includes communicating our sentiments transparently and consciously without setting expectations. By confidently imparting our requirements and needs, we can define solid limits as a type of taking care of oneself.

One way to deal with conveying limits is to utilize "I" explanations to portray what is happening and discuss the thoughts we are encountering. We can then communicate what we might want to occur all things considered and share the constructive outcomes of the new circumstance.

By laying out limits and imparting actually, we can more readily deal with our time, increment efficiency, and equilibrium work and individual life. Assigning undertakings and looking for help can help us and our associations. Assigning undertakings permits us to zero in on more elevated level liabilities, fabricate trust between colleagues, further develop correspondence, help proficiency and efficiency, and further develop using time effectively.

By assigning trivial undertakings to other people, we can zero in on our center abilities and obligations. Assigning undertakings to the perfect individuals can likewise work on the general nature of the collaboration.

Designating undertakings can likewise assist with fostering the abilities of colleagues by empowering them to assume greater liability and foster new abilities in the working environment. Confiding in partners to add to an undertaking constructs a group culture of strengthening and proceeds with a proficient turn of events.

Efficient Instruments and Innovation

A few significant instruments and computerization choices are accessible to assist with saving time and increment efficiency. These devices incorporate work hour trackers, correspondence stages, venture and assignment coordinators, booking programming, group the board frameworks, schedule applications, and brain planning instruments.

Time following apparatuses, for example, Time Specialist, can assist with following work hours precisely and distinguish regions for further development using time effectively. Correspondence stages, like Leeway, can help groups convey all the more really and lessen the requirement for tedious gatherings.

Undertaking and errand coordinators, like Trello, can help outwardly arrange assignments and ventures, making focusing on and overseeing responsibility more straightforward. Booking programming, for example, Google Schedule, can assist with planning undertakings and arrangements, guaranteeing time is utilized actually.

Utilizing these devices and robotization choices, people and associations can all the more likely oversee time, increment efficiency, and equilibrium work and individual life.

Smoothing out cycles can carry a few advantages to people and associations. These advantages incorporate expanded effectiveness, spryness, efficiency, and benefit. Smoothing out processes additionally further develops correspondence, gives more prominent perceivability into processes, saves time, kills pointless re-work, and addresses client issues.

By smoothing out processes, organizations can distinguish shortcomings and limit risk. Smoothing out processes additionally assists organizations with dissecting the results of their tasks and pursuing information driven choices. It assists organizations with saving expenses, further developing efficiency, and accomplish objectives all the more really.

Taking care of oneself and Work-Life Mix

Taking care of oneself is fundamental for both prosperity and efficiency. It decreases pressure and tension, supports our temperament, works on actual wellbeing, expands efficiency and concentration, and fabricates flexibility.

Taking part in taking care of oneself offers us a reprieve from pressure and uneasiness, permitting us to re-energize and work on the nature of our lives. Taking care of oneself exercises like breathing activities, fragrant healing, or back rubs can assist us with adapting to pressure. Taking care of oneself works on mental capabilities, permitting us to think all the more obviously and pursue better choices. It additionally gives us some alone time, empowering us to consider our necessities and needs.

Integrating taking care of oneself exercises into our routine can be testing, yet there are a few hints and methodologies to help. We can begin little and focus on taking care of oneself by finding exercises we appreciate and setting aside a few minutes for them in our day to day everyday practice.

Rehearsing self-sympathy and it is additionally crucial for be caring to ourselves. We ought to perceive our necessities and do whatever it takes to meet them without feeling remorseful or self centered.

Getting support from others, whether from companions, family, or experts, can have a tremendous effect in accomplishing our taking care of oneself objectives. Offering our taking care of oneself objectives to other people and requesting their help can be useful.

Utilizing Proficient Improvement Valuable open doors

Nonstop learning and advancement offer various advantages to people and associations, including drawing in and holding top ability, further developing representative commitment and inspiration, creating future pioneers, upgrading worker execution and efficiency, expanding income and piece of the pie, further developing client support and brand dependability, and cultivating advancement and imagination.

Besides, continuous learning advances parallel reasoning and mental adaptability, permitting people to rapidly adjust to change more. It additionally helps keep our synapses working ideally, easing back mental and memory decline as we age.

To seek after consistent learning and improvement, one can investigate different open doors like studios, courses, and industry occasions. Studios offer active preparation and functional abilities improvement in unambiguous regions. On the web or in-person courses give more top to bottom information and comprehension of a subject.

Industry occasions like meetings and workshops offer systems administration potential open doors, bits of knowledge into the most recent patterns and advancements in the field, and groundbreaking thoughts. They give amazing open doors to proficient improvement through feature talks, board conversations, and studios.

Assembling and keeping up with proficient organizations are additionally significant for development and advancement. Organizing assists people with interfacing with individuals at different expert levels, trade thoughts, increment certainty, and extend perceivability. It gives chances to professional success and helps track down ability for significant authoritative and group jobs.

Dominating using time effectively and accomplishing a solid balance between fun and serious activities is fundamental for individual and expert turn of events. It includes figuring out the difficulties, laying out clear boundaries and objectives, actually allotting time, laying out limits, appointing errands, utilizing efficient instruments and innovation, rehearsing, taking care of oneself, and making the most of expert advancement.

Carrying out the systems and strategies talked about in this article can further develop efficiency, lessen pressure, and assist you with accomplishing your ideal objectives. Recollect that accomplishing a sound balance between serious and fun activities is a continuous interaction that requires persistent exertion and consideration.

To focus on using time productively, make a steady move toward your objectives. Indeed, even little changes can have an effect over the long haul. You can begin by executing the procedures examined in this article and commend your advancement.

By laying out clear boundaries and objectives, actually dispensing your time, laying out limits, assigning undertakings, utilizing efficient instruments and innovation, rehearsing taking care of oneself, and making the most of expert advancement potential open doors, you can further develop efficiency, diminish pressure, and accomplish your ideal objectives.

Keep in mind, dominating using time effectively and accomplishing a sound balance between fun and serious activities is inside your range. Venture out today and execute the procedures examined in this article. You have the ability to make a satisfying and healthy lifestyle.

Productively Sorting out Your Working day

Most working days start with well meaning goals. You start the day siphoned up with a considerable rundown of tasks and a controllable inbox. Conversations, messages, and collaborators' fire bores before long disentangle what is happening. Your cautious arranging comes disintegrating down around you like an overstretched Lego building tower, leaving you home discouraged.

Be encouraged. Great preparation, focus, and diving into a product that isn't limited, despite the fact that it in some cases feels as is: your energy might break the cycle and save your honest goals. Many individuals' work lives can be seriously upset by continually moving positions or normal assortment. For that reason I 've gathered a rundown of ideas for upgrading business efficiency by appropriately sorting out your day.

In this way, I have summarized a rundown of ways of coordinating your normal business day. We should figure out how to coordinate your normal working day with us!

10 Methods for sorting out Your Business day for Most extreme Efficiency

We should be totally fair. We could be generally somewhat more useful at work. A considerable lot of us are at real fault for simply making a cursory effort, expecting to get past the day as easily as could be expected — frequently through no issue of our own. We'll see ten better strategies to arrange your days, as proposed by noticeable business experts.

With the accompanying rundown of how to design your typical working day, I'm persuaded that you will actually want to integrate these adjustments into your ordinary timetable to capitalize on your days.

1. Make a Normal working day Timetable and Stick

Fruitful people all have one normal component; they make a typical business day plan and their work day practices to diminish the probability of an unfavorable occasion surprising them. Individuals by and large take stops to light up their temperament. Thus, before you participate in futile side interests, make a plan for the day of work efficiency tips that incorporates all of your business related errands. To be more proficient, you may likewise carve out opportunities for each work if possible.

2. Consistently, Develop an Objective Attitude

Note that the antiquated saying, "Any street will lead you there on the off chance that you don't have the foggiest idea where you're going." That is right, and it might likewise be summed up to targets! Consistently, as a component of your general masterful course of action, put forth strategic objectives. Day to day objectives are an incredible strategy to monitor your advancement while you work for bigger targets.

3. Balance Between Many Undertakings

Adhering to a solitary work can get dreary for efficiency improvement, particularly in the event that the time has come. Moreover, such obligations force individuals to enjoy longer reprieves than are needed. It lessens efficiency and adds to how much time is spent. You can rearrange between things to keep yourself from burning through an excessive amount of time.

4. Significant Errands Ought to Never be Put-Off

Many individuals have the affinity of conceding exercises, particularly those that they dread, until some other time. It's their technique for keeping away from a troublesome yet fundamental task. Along these lines, instead of contemplating that work the entire day, it's desirable to move on immediately. You ought to finish all your significant undertakings first in a useful work area arrangement.

5. Your Current circumstance Will Impact Your Work Efficiency

An association's proficiency is its spine. It might come down to the arrangement and environment of your work areas expecting you to want your staff to be more valuable. Notwithstanding the region, consider redoing the arrangement of office furniture and equipment. You should coordinate your work area for efficiency.

6. You Ought to Get A Plant

Having a great many plants in the workplace assists with purging the air and urges representatives to be more dynamic and imaginative. More plant life in workplaces has been demonstrated to help a business day plan for logical examinations. Plants offer a few advantages, going from pressure decrease to expanded efficiency and imagination.

7. Give Your Gadgets a Spot to Call Home

Cellphones, workstations, and other electronic gadgets can assist you with keeping up with association and efficiency, however they could likewise be significant time killers. Possessing a trade for gadgets and passing on them would be the best technique to forestall fooling around in efficiency the executives.

8. Keep Your Workspace Clean

You're unquestionably not finishing a lot of work in the event that you're sitting in an untidy spot contemplating how terrible it is and the way in which you ought to clean it. Tidy up your workstation consistently for a couple of moments. You might accomplish this by dispensing with superfluous articles and adhering to whichever authoritative framework turns out best for you.

9. Begin Customizing Your Work area

Redoing your work area with some restraint might assist you with feeling all the more genuinely associated with your work, yet you should be mindful so as not to allow the extraordinary elements to become jumbling. You can include your family photograph at the edge of your work area table, or you can zest things up by adding splendid tones.

10. Integrate Innovative Progressions into Your Everyday Daily practice

For a useful day at work, the utilization of simulated intelligence acknowledgment devices to save composing time, Slack and Trello for project arranging, refreshing to various working frameworks from Windows to Macintosh, or introducing more grounded security safeguards to permit inconvenience free perusing on the Web through VPNs are only a couple of the mechanical advances.

For expanded efficiency at work, many vocations need the utilization of inventiveness. It isn't not difficult to concoct clever fixes on the off chance that you don't have a dream, a reason, or a procedure. A few people feel that levelheadedness and inventiveness are inconsistent together. Indeed, even the most normal people might think of novel answers for issues. Assuming that you're feeling creatively restrained, your psyche and body might be letting you know that you really want to make a stride back and reconsider what is happening.

It's not intense how to structure your day or how to sort out your day at work since getting ready ahead is the way to a useful day. Thus, after every day, set out a couple of moments to orchestrate your obligations as a whole. Set up an arrangement that will direct you through the urgent undertakings in general. So you'll be working savvy while every other person is really buckling down.

CHAPTER 4:

Effective Networking

Pretty much every work searcher has heard or perused that systems administration is a compelling, if not basic, part in a pursuit of employment. Vocation counsels and quest for new employment specialists will let you know that between sixty to the vast majority of all occupation associations are made through systems administration. History has exhibited many times that the main apparatus utilized in making fruitful work associations is a viable educational meeting. This page will talk about that screening exhaustively, yet first find opportunity to comprehend the rudiments behind the meeting.

To comprehend powerful systems administration we ought to initially scatter some normal systems administration fantasies.

- Compelling systems administration isn't asking individuals for a task. Running against the norm, it is centered around trading data where the two players have a potential chance to benefit.

- Organizing isn't selling. Selling will be selling. The best organizers pursue recognizing chances to help other people address issues or take care of issues, frequently through references instead of a deal. These mutually advantageous connections establish a climate where the other individual really anticipates follow-up contacts, normally on the grounds that they benefit from the discussion. The corresponding relationship will yield adequate deals potential open doors.

- **Organizing isn't only for social butterflies.** Organizing is more about tuning in than talking. A great many people in business would rather not hear your story. They need to take care of their concerns and develop their business. By listening you will reveal genuine instead of assumed open doors.

- Organizing isn't centered around getting your card or resume before everybody so particularly that whatever number individuals as could reasonably be expected hear your story. Allude to the past dispersed fantasies.

- The speed of business today is quick, yet not excessively quick to contribute time organizing. Market constraints are driving associations to become less fatty and to zero in on their center business. Subsequently associations see more prominent need than any time in recent memory to make serious answers for their clients. Keeping a laid out organization will assist you with responding to arising needs more rapidly.

- Some accept that systems administration requires an excess of time to yield wanted results. Associations and their chiefs really save time over the long haul by pre-screening possible accomplices and sources.

Systems administration can help you:

- **Figure out how and where others are utilizing your certificate.** Use the "Track down an Aggie" apparatus to distinguish other Previous Understudies that have procured tantamount degrees in your field. Search for the assortments of occupations held by those Aggies.

- **Investigate and affirm results from Vocation Appraisals.** Assuming your work experience is restricted and you wish to investigate your choices, appraisal apparatuses can give you proposals of professional fields or sorts of occupations that line up with your assets and aptitudes.

Utilize the "Track down an Aggie" data set as well as the hunt apparatuses in CareerBeam and Symplicity to recognize people in the work environment that are performing position that match those suggestions.

- **Grow your profundity of information by asking numerous individuals playing out a task you would like.** As you limit your rundown of occupations of interest, utilize the "Track down an Aggie" data set, as well as the CareerBeam and Symplicity search devices to extend your point of view of those positions by talking to more individuals in your objective regions. Realize what they like and dislike about their positions. See what encounters and viewpoints are broadly shared and what viewpoints are individually explicit.

- **Request exhortation, thoughts and references through Instructive Meetings.** Target people in the kinds of positions, ventures or associations, to assist you with growing an organization of contacts that can assist you with seeing association explicit requirements, recognize valuable open doors where associations need to develop their groups, and to expect to arise markets.

Fundamental Systems administration Rules

Organizing is in excess of a pursuit of employment. It is a functioning correspondence process that includes connecting with assistance you gain knowledge in regards to the next individual's exercises, interests, requirements, points of view and contacts. A fundamental ability ought to be intentionally figured out how to keep up with, or more significant, to impel an effective vocation. Organizing frequently brings about long haul mutual benefit connections that are both individual and expert.

The vast majority are centered around their own requirements and interests instead of your targets. To connect with and gain from others, regard their time and draw data you really want by gaining according to data and viewpoints that are mean quite a bit to them. It is astonishing the potential open doors one can uncover while tuning in.

The best organizers think outward as opposed to internal. They center after understanding the individual with whom they are drawing in while connecting for significant references as much as the fast association.

Viable systems administration happens at casual social or industry get-togethers along with all the more officially mentioned balanced arrangements. Continuously have a prepared stockpile of business cards to share contact data and to make notes of key things of interest or responsibilities that you might make during a discussion.

We could fill a page with potential systems administration contacts. Treat everybody you meet as a possible wellspring of data that could prompt your next association.

Brilliant work searchers spend roughly 75 to 80 percent of their time setting out open doors to meet individuals and direct instructive meetings. They want to take advantage of the "covered up work market" where most occupations are filled. Occupations in the "covered up market" won't be publicized and are uncovered by references and verbal.

It is probable you have known about The Aggie Organization. Endeavor to interface with, yet regard this asset. Aggies will generally have an exceptional association drawn from shared encounters and all the more significantly our common fundamental beliefs, every one of which is esteemed in business. As a result of these common qualities, a significant number of the more than 300,000 living Previous Understudies will make time to assist you with your hunt. Recollect however that the Aggie Ring you gladly wear might assist you with getting a meeting, yet there are no certifications for a task. Make it a highlight interface with your nearby A&M Club. There are more than 225 Clubs around the world. Houston, Dallas, and Austin have Aggie organizing bunches that can uphold your endeavors. If you have any desire to establish an ideal connection with most Previous Understudies stay current with the Aggie sports page.

You owe it to individuals you meet to be current on current undertakings, make time to survey the Money Road Diary and different sources to be familiar on key occasions and industry patterns.

The Instructive Meeting

Lay out a rundown of contacts to contact for a chance for an educational meeting. Confirm the name of the individual you might want to contact (on the off chance that it's anything but a reference). Recollect that names like Sam or Alex are not really orientation explicit.

Call or send an email to set up the instructive meeting. To act as an illustration of a solicitation for the meeting think about a variety of the accompanying:

"Hello, my name is _____. I'm a Previous Understudy of Texas A&M, and I'm keen on more deeply studying vocations and necessities inside the _____ business. I found your contact data while exploring the "Track down An Aggie" catalog on The Relationship of Previous Understudy's AggieNetwork.com site. Would you have a second to share guidance and thoughts with respect to your association and the _____ business.
Much thanks to you for your help.
Name
Telephone Number
Note: In the event that you call to set up an arrangement and you get voice message, Utilize a similar presentation message and leave a particular day and time that you will get back to.

Arrangements

Audit the fundamental arrangements for interviews. A similar standard procedures for new employee screenings apply to enlightening meetings with one significant exemption. Certainly don't inquire as to whether they have any openings. You requested an amazing chance to hear their recommendation, points of view and thoughts; you didn't request a chance for self-advancement. Plan for your fundamental starter discussion focuses:

Express gratitude toward them for their time. Be ready to share why you are amped up for investigating their industry and advancing more according to their points of view. Notice your reference on the off chance that you got one. They might get some information about your experience.

Be ready with a thirty-second presentation that expounds on your experience and interest. For instance:
"The previous summer, while working at _(organization name), I developed a strong

interest in the _(industry)_ and had the wonderful opportunity to collaborate with the _(job type)___ Chief. Her work gave a potential chance to have an effect with the association and it truly interested me. She worked with all parts of (obligation) and (obligation); she was earnestly keen on aiding her group _(goal)_. I preferred the assortment in her work and the way that she was an extremely certain impact at _(organization name) ."

Starting here on, recollect that your center is to clarify pressing issues, tune in and learn. Recall that your contact is the master. Remember to send a Card to say thanks that prior night heading to sleep, to ensure it is ideal.

Instructive Inquiries Questions:

How did you arrive at your current position?

What qualities/abilities make for a decent _____?

(this is the very thing that they are searching for on resumes)

How might you portray the way of life of your association?

Assuming you were beginning your vocation today, what might you do any other way?

How might I make myself more attractive?

Where do you see opportunity regions? Needs?

What different associations could you suggest that I investigate?

Who else would it be advisable for me to converse with?

What counsel would you offer to assist somebody with loving me get ready ?

Keep a Systems administration Log:

Organization or Association: Address:
Date of Meeting or Contact: Reference Source:
Central issues I Learned:

Ideas from Contact:
Much thanks to You Letter Sent:
Recommended Contacts:
Subsequent stages:

Expect needs, develop your client base, and keep your work.

Organizing doesn't stop once you secure some work. The working environment is continually evolving. Numerous items and administrations become old or are supplanted by new contributions. You will discover that all positions are transitory. You should continually show worth and assist your association with developing to remain cutthroat and to get your place as a required colleague.

Contribute the time expected to keep up with your organization to recognize recent fads, to expect needs, and to constantly be at the perfect locations brilliantly to answer open doors. A critical component to keeping up with your organization will include distinguishing and sending articles of interest or prompting your contacts to help them serve and develop their association. Most will give back in kind.

Associating for Professional success

Building proficient associations is one of the most important vocation abilities for an expert to have. A solid organization can assist you with tracking down vocation potential open doors and succeed inside them, because of your contacts' help or direction. Figuring out how to fabricate associations is an expertise that you can foster by grasping the best strategies and trying them. In this article, we talk about this expertise and why it's significant, then, at that point, list 10 hints to assist you with building associations effectively.

What's the significance here to fabricate associations?

Building associations happens when you structure a bond with someone else. While you might make individual and expert connections, both can help your expert profession. Associations permit you to profit from the assistance you get from others, and you can likewise offer help to them when they need it. These connections make a commonly useful framework, in which expanding your organization likewise builds your viability and support in proficient settings.

For what reason is it critical to construct associations?

Building associations is significant on the grounds that it makes you more adaptable. At the point when you experience tough spots, you have an organization of people who can assist with recognizing arrangements or in any case support you. Accordingly, this organization might expand your professional stability and your vertical versatility potential. For instance, in the event that you lose your employment, you can contact individuals from your organization to find out about employment opportunities or associate with people they know in your industry.

Advantages of building associations

As you grow your expert organization, you might see the various advantages of doing as such. A portion of the top motivations to deal with building more and more grounded connections include:

New position potential open doors

Proficient associations are a fantastic method for tracking down new vocation open doors. These people can educate you concerning employment opportunities, including inward situations at their association not posted openly. They're likewise useful while going after jobs since they can give proposals or act as references for you as an up-and-comer.

Mentorship connections

At the point when you structure areas of strength for an accomplished proficient in your field, it gives a chance to learn and get to the next level. You benefit from their involvement with your calling, empowering you to foster your expert abilities while trying not to commit the errors they made. At the point when you foster abilities and information with their assistance, it can support your presentation at work.

Expanded advancement

Developing your organization likewise empowers you to create as an expert in light of the fact that these associations can educate or move you to construct your abilities and information. Additionally, large numbers of the best techniques for developing your organization set you in places to propel yourself, like going to gatherings, studios and other expert occasions. Making a move to propel your abilities and vocation can show your obligation to proficient turn of events and your profession, which businesses frequently appreciate.

Extended customers

Creating bonds with potential clients is an extraordinary method for building unwaveringness. At the point when your client feels they have a special interaction with you, they're bound to contemplate the administrations you give. This appreciation might lead them to prescribe you to their companions and friends, assisting you with developing your client base.

Quicker advancement
Interfacing with more ranking staff individuals at your organization can assist with expanding your chances for advancement. In the event that these people have a current, positive relationship with you, they definitely know and value what you can do. This information can make them more ready to put your name forward for an advancement or track down ways of assisting you with progressing inside the association.

10 successful ways of building associations, to propel your vocation:
In spite of the fact that associations can grow normally, that doesn't mean there aren't ways of

working on the viability of these endeavors to assemble them. These tips can assist you with making more grounded bonds while making proficient associations:

1. Partake in your industry

By partaking in proficient associations or going to meetings connected with your calling, you get close enough to a wide scope of experts in your field. These exercises address incredible chances to associate with companions and more senior industry experts. Proficient associations and meetings frequently offer more relaxed occasions other than formal ones, furnishing you with additional chances to fabricate unique interactions and more grounded bonds.

2. Be active

While this attribute might come all the more normally to social butterflies, thoughtful people can view open doors as friendly and draw in with others. Find leisure activities or occasions that urge you to cooperate with new individuals. Regardless of whether it's not straightforwardly connected with your work, you can in any case meet individuals who can in any case serve important jobs in your expert organization. You can likewise work on being active in your everyday existence by driving yourself to make casual banter or take part in discussions with your associates more regularly. The more you practice this ability, the more agreeable you'll feel.

3. Lay out various styles of contact

While interfacing with someone else, laying out various techniques for communication is useful. For instance, you can trade telephone numbers and email addresses while meeting somebody. This strategy expands the quantity of ways you can contact when important and can assist you with laying out correspondence inclinations. Assuming you want to reach each other about significant circumstances, you could call or text, for instance. Then you can utilize messages to perform essential relationship upkeep and send easygoing messages or correspondences to one another.

4. Track down shared traits

While attempting to interface with someone else, finding shared interests or obligations can give a simple wellspring of conversation. These interests can be proficient or individual. For instance, during a new employee screening, you might make reference to the recruiting director that you went to a similar college as them. These shared characteristics can offer a solid groundwork for connections since they furnish you with bits of knowledge into one another.

5. Offer some incentive

Whether individual or expert, the best connections have a cooperative bond where the two members give advantages to one another. At the point when it becomes imbalanced, one individual might feel like the relationship isn't quite as certifiable as they would like. Assuming you demand help from somebody, show them you're willing to offer your help or backing when they need it. This eagerness makes a more adjusted relationship that features your veritable regard and worry for one another.

6. Show your appreciation

One of the easiest ways of causing somebody to feel appreciated is to offer your thanks after they help you out. At the point when individuals feel appreciated or esteemed, it urges them to keep keeping up with and reinforcing the relationship. Contingent upon the circumstance, you can express it face to face or send a note, email or gift to communicate your much obliged. These activities show you perceive the worth the individual gave to you and that you're appreciative for their liberality.

7. Distribute your work

You can exploit industry diaries or publish content to a blog stage to get seen by individuals in your field. By distributing your work, you make it accessible for others to access and share. People who read your work and find it intriguing or beneficial may reach you to share their contemplations or in any case associate with you. While it might require work to make an article, video or other distributed works, this strategy permits you to trust that similar people will reach you instead of attempting to track down them yourself.

8. Foster a web-based presence

From virtual entertainment stages to an individual site, fostering a web-based presence is one more method for interfacing with different experts. You can understand industry sites or thought pioneers on different stages and take part in web-based discussions via virtual entertainment or expert gatherings. These stages empower you to find and share assets to help each other and assemble bonds. Whenever the situation allows, share your virtual entertainment profiles or expert site with others. They can get in touch with you through these locales and find out about you, both by and by and as far as the work you do.

9. Go about as a host

Arranging and facilitating occasions can be an incredible method for meeting individuals and structure bonds with them. Whenever you work with an industry occasion or make an industry bunch, it places you as a resource for people keen on taking part. They might reach you previously or after the occasion with questions or remarks, permitting you to lay out connections. At the point when you center around occasions or gatherings connected with your industry, it empowers you to track down similar people and possibly helps lead to proficient open doors.

10. Registration with significant contacts

Subsequent to building an underlying association, you really want to keep investing amounts of energy toward keeping up with the relationship. You may particularly need to consider this strategy to assist you with keeping significant contacts, like clients or guides. Registration exercises can change from remembering your contacts for your vacation card records to sending a short email when you haven't represented a lengthy period to get up to speed with your lives or examine proficient open doors. Putting forth these attempts shows you esteem the relationship and helps keep you at the front of their psyche.

Fundamental parts of building associations

You can find a few normal qualities present in serious areas of strength for most. Understanding these parts can assist you evaluate and foster your associations with others. Basic parts serious areas of strength for of include:

- **Realness:** It's valuable to foster connections in view of genuine bonds. This realness makes further connections since you know one another's actual characters and foundations, frequently making it simpler to keep up with your relationship later on.

- **Normal reason:** Solid connections frequently happen where the members share normal causes or interests. Sharing something for all intents and purpose makes it more straightforward to create and keep up with affinity.

- **Consistency:** When the two players feel that they can precisely foresee how the other will respond or answer in a circumstance, this is an indication of consistency. This degree of consistency can assist with causing more grounded bonds in light of the fact that the two players feel they can depend on one another.

- **Correspondence:** With correspondence, the two players help and back one another. Since everybody benefits from this complementary relationship, they're bound to need to proceed with it.

107

CHAPITRE 5:

STRONG COMMUNICATION

One of the foundations of a successful business is a leader's ability to communicate clearly and effectively with employees, within teams, and across the organization.

And, with hundreds of various communication platforms, fully or partially remote teams, and even multicultural teams spanning many time zones in today's complicated and rapidly evolving corporate environment, efficient communication has never been more important—or more difficult.

As a result, the capacity to communicate may be the most important quality for a manager.

The good news is that these abilities can be taught and mastered.

These eight suggestions will help you improve your communication abilities for the benefit of your business and career.

1. Be precise and succinct.

Word choice is the most crucial component of communication. In terms of wording, less is more.

When writing or speaking, the keys to effective and persuasive communication are clarity and, when possible, brevity.

Define your goals and your audience before engaging in any sort of communication.

Outlining what you want to express and why can assist you guarantee that you include all necessary information. It will also help you get rid of unnecessary things.

Avoid superfluous words and flowery language, which can detract from your point.

And, while repetition may be important in some circumstances, do it with caution and sparingly. Repeating your message ensures that it is received, but too much repetition can cause them to tune out.

2. Plan ahead of time

Before you start any form of conversation, plan out what you're going to say and how you're going to say it.

Being prepared, however, entails more than merely preparing a presentation.

Taking into account the entire communication, from start to finish, is another aspect of preparation. Look into the data you might need to support your message. Think about how you answer inquiries and critiques. Try to plan for the unexpected.

Prepare a list of concrete instances of your employee's behavior to support your evaluation before a performance review, for example.

Know exactly what you want before engaging in a wage or promotion discussion. Be ready to talk about compromises and ranges; be aware of what you will and won't accept. And keep specific statistics on hand to back up your argument, such as applicable salary for your role and region (but make sure your research is based on publicly available data, not company rumor or anecdotal evidence).

Before you start a conversation, think about probable questions, requests for more information or clarification, and arguments so you can answer them calmly and clearly.

3. Pay attention to nonverbal communication.

More information can be communicated through our body language, gestures, and facial expressions than through our words.

Nonverbal cues can have up to 93 percent more influence than spoken words. If the two are in disagreement, we are more prone to believe nonverbal signs over spoken statements.

Leaders must be particularly skilled at understanding nonverbal signs.

Employees who are hesitant to express their differences or worries, for example, may exhibit their uneasiness by crossing their arms or refusing to make eye contact. You may be able to adapt your communication strategies if you are aware of others' body language.

Leaders need to be able to simultaneously regulate their own nonverbal cues.

Your nonverbal cues should always support your message. At best, contradictory verbal and nonverbal cues can be confusing. At worst, it can derail your message and damage your team's trust in you, your organization, and even yourself.

4. Be mindful of your tone
It's not always as important what you say as it is how you say it. Your tone, like other nonverbal indicators, may either add power and emphasis to your message or completely destroy it.

In workplace disagreements and confrontation, tone can be extremely critical. A carefully chosen term with a favorable connotation fosters goodwill and confidence. A badly chosen term with ambiguous or negative meanings can easily lead to confusion.

Tone in speech comprises volume, projection, intonation, and word choice. It might be difficult to regulate tone in real time to ensure that it reflects your intent. However, being aware of your tone can allow you to adjust it appropriately if a communication appears to be going in the wrong direction.

When writing, tone can be more easily controlled. Remembering the tone and message of your communication, make sure to read it at least once. If doing so does not violate confidentially, you may want to read it aloud or have a trusted colleague read it over.

And, if you're having a passionate debate via email or another textual medium, don't be too quick to respond.

If at all feasible, write your response but wait a day or two before sending it. Re-reading your communication after your emotions have calmed down often helps you to adjust your tone in a way that is less likely to aggravate the conflict. 5. Engage in active listening.

5. Communication almost always involves two or more people.
When it comes to communicating effectively, listening is just as crucial as speaking. Listening, on the other hand, can be more difficult than we realize.

Communication expert Marjorie North explains in her blog post Mastering the Basics of Communication that we only hear around half of what the other person says during any given interaction.

The purpose of active listening is to guarantee that you receive the complete message, not just the words the person is saying. Here are some active listening examples:

- focusing solely on the speaker and paying them attention

Getting rid of distractions, judgments, and counter-arguments in your thoughts.

- Resisting the want to interject your own opinions.

Using open, affirming body language to stay engaged and demonstrate to the speaker that you are paying attention

When responding, restate or paraphrase what you've heard.

Pose open-ended inquiries meant to extract more details.

6. Enhance your emotional discernment

Emotional intelligence is the cornerstone of communication. Put simply, you cannot effectively interact with people until you are able to recognize, evaluate, and comprehend your own feelings.

According to Margaret Andrews' essay on How to Increase Your Emotional Intelligence, "you can begin to manage these emotions and behaviors if you're aware of your own emotions and the behaviors they trigger."

It will come naturally to leaders with high emotional intelligence to utilize positive body language, maintain proper tone, and participate in active listening.

Emotional intelligence comprises more than just knowing how to control and understand your own feelings. Empathy for others is the other component, which is just as crucial for successful communication.

For example, having an empathic talk with an employee might ease a stressful situation.

Even though you might still need to break terrible news to them, you can help to ease their hurt feelings or prevent misunderstandings by carefully listening to their point of view and demonstrating your comprehension of it.

7. Create a communication plan for the workplace

In the modern workplace, information is always being exchanged in a multitude of formats. Each and every communication needs to be interpreted within the framework of that more extensive informational flow.

Without a workplace communication plan, even the most skilled communicator could struggle to get their point through.

A communication strategy is the framework that governs the exchange of information between your company and its customers. It can—and ought to—define what and how you interact with stakeholders, managers, staff members, and consumers.

Your plan should address, at the very least, who receives what message when. This guarantees that the right information is given to everyone at the appropriate moment.

It can be as specific as how you communicate, down to specifying which kinds of tools you use for certain kinds of information. You may choose, for instance, whether the entire team or company should use a group chat or whether a meeting should have been described in an email. This kind of fundamental guidance can help to organize information flow. It will make sure that everyone has access to the information they require and that crucial information isn't obscured by unimportant stuff.

8. Establish a favorable company culture

Effective communication also heavily depends on the organizational culture in which you are communicating.

Communication will be simpler and more efficient in general in a pleasant work atmosphere that is built on open communication, openness, trust, and empathy.

If employees have faith in their management, they will be more open to hearing what they have to say. Additionally, if managers encourage their staff members to speak up, make recommendations, and even offer constructive criticism of their own, it will be simpler for them to gain buy-in and even offer constructive critique.

According to Lorne Rubis, "The most dangerous organization is a silent one" (Six Tips for Building a Better Workplace Culture). Only in a culture based on psychological safety and trust can communication be successful in both directions.

Suggestions and criticisms from authoritative bosses who close themselves off to outsiders, don't accept responsibility for their actions, and don't provide information are likely to be treated with defensiveness or outright rejection.

Even the tiniest communication can be misinterpreted, resulting in misunderstandings and needless conflict, if trust and transparency are lacking.

There will always be difficulties when it comes to communicating with coworkers and colleagues. There will inevitably be miscommunications and misconceptions that need to be cleared up, and regrettably, sometimes corporate messaging don't say what we want to hear—particularly in trying times.

However, developing and becoming an expert communicator will ease your leadership responsibilities, especially in trying situations. It will undoubtedly be time well spent to invest in developing these abilities.

Upgrading Your Relational Abilities

Work explicit abilities have consistently had a put on the resume, however businesses progressively underscore the significance of relational abilities. Also, for good explanation. Indeed, even the most secluded of individual patrons should have the option to interface with others. And keeping in mind that these abilities are basic to outcome in our singular jobs, the impacts aren't restricted to our sets of expectations. Solid relational abilities can assist you with succeeding at work, team up with others, and even establish a better workplace.

There's no question that our specialized abilities are basic with regards to going about our responsibilities competently. In any case, odds are great that there's more than one individual who went to a similar school, procured a similar confirmation, or dominated a similar range of abilities. While you're employing for an open job in your group, what separates work searchers? Is it their knowledge or their behavior?

You got it: relational abilities. We should get into what they are and the way in which they can assist different groups and people with succeeding.

What are relational abilities in the working environment?

Taking everything into account, we associate with others at work, two things stick out: how gifted the individual is at their job, and how we feel subsequent to conversing with them. The main measure is specialized abilities, and the subsequent measure is relational abilities.

What are relational abilities?

Relational abilities are the manners by which we associate with our collaborators, chiefs, clients, and act at work. Those with solid relational abilities will quite often be more innovative, more powerful colleagues, appreciate work more, and add to a positive workplace.

The business case for relational abilities

You probably went through years preparing to be great at what you do — however odds are great that nobody in your scholastic profession invested as much energy preparing you to have great relational abilities. So what difference do they make to such an extent? Are relational abilities vital in the work environment and in your vocation?

Managers are truly employing for here and there, relational abilities. Presently, saying this doesn't imply that that work explicit abilities aren't significant. Numerous jobs require a particular range of abilities or long periods of involvement (our thought process of as "hard abilities"). However, in any event, when questioners are centered around abilities based recruiting, there's just such an excess of mastery that can be conveyed during an employing cycle.

Then again, progress in new employee screenings depends vigorously on relational abilities — frequently called "delicate abilities." These can't be measured, yet their effect can be felt in each association. Whether these characteristics are a vital piece of the job, the conventional screening rewards the individuals who can tune in, convey, answer questions, and even giggle at the right jokes.

Great correspondence and relational abilities likewise go far post-interview. When you're in your job, your relational abilities will decide if you fabricate connections during onboarding and how quick you get on assumptions. It's a calculate whether you make companions at work and how quick you get advanced. Beside that, it likewise straightforwardly affects the nature of work you do — particularly assuming your job relies upon compelling correspondence with others.

There are different relational abilities that individuals need to have — or create — to find success in the working environment. Here are a few that businesses esteem across various jobs:

Kinds of relational abilities at work
There's no question that each job requires an equilibrium of relational abilities to find success. Notwithstanding, the specific sort of abilities might differ across occupations, groups, and work environments. Here are a few normal

relational abilities that have a constructive outcome at work:

1. Relational abilities

At the first spot on the list is relational abilities — both composed and verbal. To grasp assumptions, express needs, and team up really, representatives should have the option to discuss well with others. Regardless of your job or industry, associations have long seen the benefit of further developing relational abilities. A few instances of these skills include:

Undivided attention

By certain evaluations, just around 10% of individuals listen successfully or recall any critical measure of what we hear. Consider your last gathering. Assuming it included ten individuals, that implies just a single individual removed anything of importance.

Working on your capacity to listen effectively can assist with raising efficiency, decrease false impressions, and work on your associations with

125

others. You'll turn into the individual who's ready to review the extraordinary thoughts from a meeting to generate new ideas or get the group in the groove again after an interference.

Composing

It just so happens, our teachers were correct — composing is a fundamental expertise for pretty much every expert. Especially in crossover and remote workplaces, you might find that you spend a critical piece of your day drafting reminders, messages, introductions, and, surprisingly, Slack messages. Solid composing abilities can likewise assist you with making your resume and introductory letter captivate everyone.

Non-verbal communication

Frequently alluded to as nonverbal correspondence, many positions don't remember to put expertise in perusing non-verbal communication high on the rundown. Nonetheless, implicit correspondence is a fundamental piece of discussing successfully with others. Having the option to get on non-verbal signals can straightforwardly affect the primary concern — especially in jobs like deals.

2. Training abilities

While there are numerous ways of being a pioneer, not every one of them include overseeing others — however practically every one of them include training. Whether you're a group chief or individual benefactor, you'll probably wind up aiding others inside your specialty or group. Those with a training initiative style will quite often be more cooperative, intrigued by others, sympathetic, and great communicators.

Tutoring

Creating tutor mentee connections in your group is one of the single most noteworthy ventures you can make in vocation improvement. Coaches speed up the profession development of their mentees — further developing having a place, work fulfillment, and maintenance.

However, the tutor mentee relationship is an exceptionally relational one essentially. In that capacity, the two players need fantastic relational abilities to benefit from it.

Input

Maybe one of the most significant (and alarming) relationship building abilities to create is the capacity to give input. In any case, while we as a whole realize that we benefit from getting criticism, we frequently stress over how it will be gotten by others. Workers that are sure about both giving and getting criticism are many times impetuses for positive development in their groups.

Affirmation

Many individuals decide to work with a mentor for expanded responsibility and backing in hitting objectives. But on the other hand it's one of the most fulfilling portions of dealing with a group. A genuine cooperative person can share credit, remembering others for their commitments and endeavors. This sort of acknowledgment can change work connections and representative fulfillment.

3. The capacity to understand anyone on a deeper level

Our capacity to appreciate anyone on a profound level, or close to home remainder — is our capacity to comprehend and control our own feelings, as well as grasp the feelings of others. EQ is quite possibly of the main relational expertise, as it straightforwardly affects work environment connections. At the point when our capacity to understand individuals on a profound level is high, we will quite often coexist better with others, have a superior balance between serious and fun activities, and move toward work with a superior disposition. Some center capacity to appreciate anyone on a profound level abilities include:

Compassion

Compassion implies that we comprehend and relate to the sensations of others. Sympathetic people will more often than not be innately gifted at perusing looks and getting on the "vibe" in a room. They recall insights concerning others and are great at building connections.

Mindfulness

You may be shocked to discover that it's more difficult to precisely measure your own sentiments than it is to understand others. Those with high ability to understand anyone on a deeper level, be that as it may, can get on changes in their own sentiments, and even distinguish what set off them. Creating mindfulness makes you a superior chief, yet it assists you with understanding yourself better. You gain a more profound comprehension of the whole wheel of feelings, in addition to a select and strong few.

Humor

A funny bone — particularly working — has numerous unmistakable advantages. Humor in the working environment increments union, diminishes pressure, assists colleagues with holding quicker, and makes refereeing more straightforward. Finding the tomfoolery in work works on both your experience and the experience of others in the working environment. It's simpler to come to work with an uplifting perspective when you live it up doing what you do.

3 methods for creating relational abilities at work

Whether you're a pioneer, chief, work searcher (or the entirety of the abovementioned), you'll need to make constant improvements in your relational abilities. It's similarly as significant — and worth the same amount of devotion — as formal preparation and upskilling in your profession. Here are a few plans to remember to fabricate relational abilities for yourself (and for your workers):

1. Lead with deference

Maybe the main way you can fabricate an establishment for good associations with others is to lead with deference. Accept that each individual is giving a valiant effort. Particularly working, everybody wins when every individual succeeds, so it merits assuming the best about others. This mentality enables collaboration and velocities compromise.

2. Move toward work with humor

You don't need to tell wisecracks relentless, however it's really smart to carry a little levity to your work. Having some good times increments social association and lifts imagination — and it goes quite far towards building mental wellbeing.

3. Meet with a mentor

Epitomizing solid relational characteristics in a vacuum is quite difficult. Working with a mentor gives a sort of sandbox where you can manage (and get criticism on) your abilities as you construct them. A mentor can assist you with creating solid listening abilities, have good expectations about open talking, and pretend troublesome discussions.

Tips for supervisors to foster workers' relational abilities

As directors, you can set areas of strength for a for your representatives and assist them with growing great relational abilities. Here are a few different ways you can uphold your group:

1. Dedicate time to one-on-ones

Your one-on-one gatherings are the best an open door for you to get to know your immediate reports. Adopt an instructing strategy to initiative and urge them to address you really about what they need. Survey the earlier little while and search for situations that would profit from another methodology or an instructing discussion.

2. Give ordinary input

Individuals are frequently terrified of giving input, and that is doubly evident with regards to relational abilities. All things considered, it can feel like we're evaluating their identity as individuals — which is never the objective.

While talking about relational abilities, adopt an objective strategy and keep away from judgment. Pay attention to how they feel and approach correspondence as a device to make coordinated effort and probability.

3. Be merciful

Creating relational abilities is difficult — and truth be told, certain discussions can be out and out setting off for certain individuals. Be delicate and recollect: everybody is making an honest effort. It requires investment and a great deal of mindfulness to work on interactive abilities. Be delicate, reliable, and model solid relational abilities yourself by showing empathy. Your group will see the value in your methodology and the interest in them, too.

Last contemplations

Relational abilities and authority abilities remain closely connected. If you have
any desire to know how to help your group's efficiency, joint effort, and construct serious areas of strength for a, it won't drop by doing all

the more hard abilities preparing. Put time and assets into working in your group's (and your own!) relational abilities. More than some other expertise, it can possibly change your whole working environment culture.

CHAPTER 6:

Navigating Your Career Journey

Envision that you had your very own guide that spread out the particular advances you really want to take to get to the following objective on your vocation way. I realize it sounds unrealistic, yet I needed to stroll through how I've done this for myself on different occasions — and how you can do it as well. Exploring a profession way in the tech space can be precarious. There are times where things can move quick. There are times when things can move unquestionably leisurely. New groups spring up or vanish out of the blue. What's more, it's simply human instinct to get exhausted doing likewise again and again for an extensive stretch of time. At the point when you join these variables, it's not difficult to feel caught, and it very well may be really upsetting. I converse with such countless individuals that put off chipping away at their own vocation way since things get going or they get pushed simply mulling over everything. This is absolutely reasonable — yet you must be deliberate about saving time for you to chip away at yourself. In the age of our "treat yo self" culture, simply view at it as your expert taking care of oneself. Something that generally kept me connected with (in any event, when I was miserable in a job) was keeping my next vocation step in my sights. It seems like a straightforward idea, yet some of the time it's not exactly simple or easy. Whether it's a long haul or transient objective, having something to zero in on is as yet significant. At the point when the master plan is in your sights, it permits you to concentrate your activities in general and choices towards that following stage. In the event that you approach every day as an interest into the future you, it makes the monotonous routine worth the effort. I read an article as of late that said that individuals that have their next excursion arranged, regardless of how a long ways ahead, were for the most part more joyful. I've viewed this as a comparative idea that I've applied to my expert life. I've generally adopted a genuinely coherent strategy to moving to the subsequent stage in my own vocation way, and it's been really successful. Individuals that I have driven that have followed these means have made lucidity and progress also, so I needed to impart it to you. Actually, it's really logical — and brilliantly clear!

Here are the 7 moves toward explore your profession way:

1. Do some examination
2. Make a rundown
3. Realize that all will be well
4. Begin to fill in the spaces
5. Dive into the holes that you find
6. Get explicit
7. Make a move

1. Do some examination

Expecting you have an overall thought of which job you are pursuing, go to Glassdoor, LinkedIn, or even your own boss' vocation page and find postings that match what you're searching for. Most work postings will have a "necessities" or a "what you will bring" segment. Make a point to not simply look at one posting from one organization or even your boss' necessities. This is the information gathering step. We as a whole know that the more information, the better.

2. Make a rundown

Whenever you've accumulated two or three tantamount work postings, you ought to have an extended rundown of prerequisites. Fire up Google Drive and make another doc. Toss a table along with 2 segments and put each of the prerequisites that you gathered in the left section. (We'll finish up the right segment in sync 4.) Presently, assuming you're in any way similar to me, as of now you'll see a rundown so lengthy that the existential fear and uneasiness will set in — and you could address whether this is what you truly care about.

3. Realize that all will be well

There isn't anything in this step.

Simply slowly inhale and realize that you got this.

4. Begin to fill in the spaces

You have likely seen those correlation graphs on G2 that think about the elements of at least 2 contending programming programs. This part is somewhat similar to that — however rather than two distinct programming programs, It's simply the future you versus the ongoing you. Presently it is the right time to give yourself some credit. Go down the rundown and put a mark close to the necessities that you have insight with. I have a speedy little litmus test that I use to decide whether I feel sufficiently great to verify a prerequisite or not. It's straightforward: On the off chance that somebody requested that I share an encounter where I exhibited the particular obligation, might I at any point give explicit models? In the event that you can give explicit models, you can most likely confirm it. If not, I would leave it open.

5. Dive into the holes that you find

Now that you've filled in the spaces, you will see the glaring (or not really glaring) holes among you and the future you. The straightforwardness acquired from this exercise alone is worth the effort. These holes, however terrifying as they seem to be, engage you to be laser-centered around the moves that you can now make to draw nearer to the following stage in your profession. Since it has become so obvious what you really want to learn, now is the right time to make it happen.

6. Get explicit

Subsequent to going through that activity, you will presently have a quite certain rundown of abilities, encounters, and capabilities that stand among you and the following stage on your profession way. Here things can get overpowering, yet it doesn't need to be. I normally take every one of the required abilities, encounters, or skills and make a sub-rundown of things that I can do to dominate them. Some of them could require some instruction or affirmations, so ensure you ask your foreman or supervisor assuming that your organization offers assistance with those things. For different prerequisites, you'll observe that there are presumably things that you can do in your ongoing job to fabricate those abilities or get that experience. Here is a speedy and useful model:

Administration Abilities OR EXPERIENCE Required

- Conceivable Things to do

Public take

- the group at an enormous gathering required for everyone

- Coordinate with my chief to run a group meeting one time each month

- Partake in client confronting

occasions

- And to lead the pack in a group or division undertaking and make tasks to peers

- Peruse a book on viable designation abilities and offer it with my chief

Extreme didiscussions.

- Give my chief some immediate input

- Volunteer to impart a group cycle change

- Pretend different input

7. Make a move

Since you have a rundown of explicit things to do, it very well may be enticing to take on a lot without a moment's delay. I have consistently observed it to be best when I simply pick a couple of things to zero in on and own them prior to taking on more.

Giving yourself an opportunity to zero in on your vocation way is proficient taking care of oneself

Zeroing in on your expert advancement expects you to take time and spotlight on yourself, which can be hard for certain individuals. Furthermore, we should be genuine, on the off chance that you work in the tech space, you likely have a ceaseless heap of work to do. Help yourself out and set a few blocks of time on your schedule for

you

also,

your

improvement. You owe it to your future self.

Systems for Development and Advancement

On the off chance that you believe individuals should purchase something, you really want to educate them first. It sounds straightforward, however that is the center standard behind all advancement techniques — bringing issues to light about an item, then persuading potential clients they ought to get it. Find out around 12 unique kinds of advancement systems, in addition to best practices to think up your very own fruitful technique.

Just before 2009, Red Bull paid Robbie Maddison $2 million to fire up his bike, launch himself off an incline, and land on top of a 10-story building. Maddison nailed the trick, and Red Bull set standing as a brand stretches the boundaries of what's conceivable. Presently the organization isn't simply a caffeinated drink producer — it's a pillar of outrageous games and rousing competitors.

Individuals don't simply pick Red Bull for the taste and shock of energy it gives. On account of the brand's unmistakable advancement technique, clients lean toward the Red Bull brand since it's popular, tense, and part of something greater.

What is an advancement procedure?
An advancement procedure is an arrangement to provoke or increment interest for an item. It

frames the strategies you'll use to bring issues to light about your item and get individuals keen on getting it.

The objective of an advancement system is to acquaint likely clients with your item and persuade them to make a buy. You need to move them along the purchaser's excursion — the way clients take from understanding a need, taking into account your item as an answer, lastly choosing to purchase.

Advancement methodology as opposed to advertising system

Your advancement methodology is only one piece of a bigger showcasing system — a drawn out plan illustrating how you'll market and sell your item. A fruitful showcasing plan covers every one of the strategies you'll use to advance your item, including the full "showcasing blend": item, value, spot, and advancement. Your advancement technique is a critical part of the showcasing blend.

Here is a breakdown of the showcasing blend, otherwise called the 4 P's of promoting:

- **Item:** The thing you're selling.
- **Value:** The amount you ought to charge for your item to create a gain.

- **Place:** Where you ought to offer your item to arrive at your interest group.

- **Advancement:** How you drive interest for your item and move clients through the showcasing channel.

The fourth "P" of advertising — advancement — is your advancement technique.

- **Peruse:** Promoting as opposed to publicizing:

What's the distinction?

Advancement methodologies and the advertising pipe

The purchaser's process is much of the time pictured as a pipe partitioned into three segments: top of channel, center of pipe, and lower part of channel. Clients enter their excursion at the highest point of the pipe, then, at that point, choose to buy your item once they arrive at the base. A fruitful advancement system remembers various strategies to interest clients for each part of the promoting pipe.

Here is a breakdown of the showcasing channel, with model advancement methodologies for each part:

Top of pipe

At the point when a client is at the highest point of the pipe, they know the issue they need to tackle and are searching for an answer. They may not have the foggiest idea about your item exists yet, so at this stage your advancement methodology ought to catch the client's eye and assemble mindfulness about your image and your item.

Model advancement systems: television promotions, occasion sponsorships, content showcasing

Center of channel

In the channel, clients gauge your item against other accessible choices. To keep them in the channel, you want to show how your item is unique in relation to the opposition and persuade clients that your item is the most ideal choice. Here, your advancement technique ought to make a close to home association and demonstrate the way that your item can explicitly determine client problem areas.

Model advancement systems: Client audits, free examples, contextual investigations

Peruse: How to make a cutthroat investigation (with models)

Lower part of channel

Clients choose if they have any desire to buy your item when they're in the lower part of the channel. To target lower part of-channel clients, your advancement system ought to incite individuals to make a move.

Model advancement procedures: Unique arrangements, email offers, adaptable merchandise exchanges

12 sorts of advertising advancement methodologies, with models
There are loads of ways of advancing an item. Assuming that you're searching for motivation, we've spread out 12 unique sorts of advancement methodologies underneath.

1. Paid publicizing
Paid publicizing is many times the principal sort of advancement that rings a bell. This clear technique includes paying to show a promotion in a particular spot at a particular time, so you can catch the consideration of your objective market. It's an incredible method for building

brand mindfulness and acquaint your image with individuals who might not have known about it previously.

Here are a few instances of paid publicizing:

- TV advertisements

- Radio advertisements

- Paper and magazine advertisements

- Bulletins

- Online showcase promotions (for instance, through Google or virtual entertainment)

2. Content showcasing

Content showcasing is a typical sort of computerized advancement procedure, zeroed in on circulating important substance to draw in and hold a group of people. The thought behind happy promoting is this: It connects your image with valuable, important substance that assists clients with addressing issues — building trust over the long haul and eventually reassuring clients to purchase your items. Content showcasing is an incredible special instrument for any organization, yet it's particularly useful for organizations with longer deals cycles, as B2B and SaaS organizations. For these organizations, content advertising gives sufficient client training to purchasers to pursue informed buy choices.

Content advertising comes in many structures, including:

- Blog entries

- Recordings

- Online entertainment posts

- Email bulletins

- Web recordings

- White Papers or reports
- Content made to further develop Website design enhancement (site improvement)

what's more, outrageous competitors, all things considered. These days, sponsorships frequently incorporate web-based entertainment powerhouse showcasing — making associations with people who became popular through virtual entertainment stages like Instagram or Youtube.

The objective of a sponsorship is to support your image's public picture and validity. Falling in line with another brand can drive media openness, work on advertising, and grow your crowd — in addition to make you stand apart from the opposition.

4. Email advertising

Email advertising assists you with interfacing with your main interest group by means of — you got it — email. You can send messages to any supporters on your mailing list — whether they're expected clients, faithful clients, or in the middle between. For instance, you can gather email addresses from possible clients by offering free items or administrations in return for their data.

There are loads of things you can email, including:

- Bulletins and selective substance

- Data about item delivers

- Extraordinary arrangements and coupons

5. Retargeting

Retargeting centers around clients (or likely clients) with high buy goal. As such, it includes focusing on sections of your client base who've previously made it down to the lower part of the advertising pipe. Focusing on retargeting can assist you with getting an exceptional yield on your speculation, since this crowd is now ready to rock and roll to purchase.

For instance, retargeting could include:

- Sending update messages to clients who topped off an internet shopping basket however didn't look at.

- Showing designated notices to clients who bought your items previously.

- Sending support messages to individuals who bought something some time prior however haven't come back.

6. Reference advertising

Reference advertising is the point at which you get clients to educate their companions regarding your image. Otherwise called verbal exchange promoting, reference showcasing happens naturally when you have an incredible item — however you can likewise speed it alongside unique arrangements and impetuses for clients who allude their associations.

Reference showcasing is a strong system since it's for all intents and purposes free. Also, since individuals will quite often believe their companions, alluded clients are bound to really buy your item than somebody who simply sees a promotion. For instance, Dropbox utilized reference showcasing to for all time increment information exchanges by 60% — in the long run developing into an extravagant startup.

7. Occasion showcasing

Occasion advertising includes taking part in, supporting, or facilitating occasions to advance your image or item. This system helps you interface and draw in with clients direct, so they can get a genuine feeling of your item and what your image addresses. That, however occasions can assist you with building your image presence, create leads, and produce altruism with clients.

Occasion advertising comes in many structures, including:

- Gatherings

- Career expos

- Courses and classes

- Online classes

- Virtual occasions

- Live streaming occasions

- Local area occasions

8. Extraordinary Causes

Adjusting your image to an exceptional reason causes clients to feel like they're essential for something greater. They're not simply helping themselves by buying your items — they're likewise helping make the world a superior spot. This can assist with helping brand steadfastness and convince clients to pick your image over rivals.

The dress organization Patagonia is an incredible illustration of this. By advancing their maintainable assembling processes, Patagonia draws in and holds clients who have faith in ecological protection.

9. Client surveys

Client surveys are one of the most impressive showcasing instruments out there. Brands like Amazon, Howl, and TripAdvisor constructed their organizations out of audits — creating trust by advancing client criticism. The magnificence of this methodology is that it urges clients to advance your image for you. What's more, the same length as you have an excellent item (and positive surveys), this kind of client created content can go far in persuading expected clients to buy.

Gathering client audits frequently happens naturally, however you can speed it along by explicitly mentioning surveys from current clients by means of email or site flags. Some more current brands likewise seed audits by sending items to clients in return for their genuine criticism.

10. Client steadfastness programs

Client steadfastness programs reward individuals who over and again interface with your image. It's a method for keeping clients returning by offering arrangements, limits, and elite item dispatches. The more clients buy from your organization, the more advantages they acquire. For instance, the excellence organization Sephora advances a faithfulness program that offers limits and gifts to clients who spend a specific sum.

Reliability programs don't simply support client maintenance — they additionally assist with persuading likely purchasers to pick your image over rivals. By advancing devotion programs, you show ways clients can set aside cash and get all the more bang from their buck over the long run.

11. Free examples, giveaways, and preliminaries

Everybody adores free stuff. Offering tests of your item can assist with advancing consumer loyalty and cause clients to feel like they're getting an extraordinary arrangement. Be that as it may, in particular, free examples and preliminaries give potential clients direct involvement in your item — and subsequently the certainty to really get it later on.

To utilize this advancement technique, organizations can:

- **Offer a time for testing so clients can evaluate the item risk free.** Rec centers, applications, and online programming organizations frequently do this.

- **Offer free examples for clients who visit stores face to face.** The distribution center club Costco is renowned for utilizing this technique.

- **Incorporate free examples when clients buy an item.** This technique can urge existing clients to attempt new items. For instance, online magnificence providers like Glossier frequently incorporate free skincare and cosmetics tests with each buy.

- **Coordinate challenges with free awards.** This is an effective method for gathering reaching data from expected clients. For instance, an inn organization could urge possible clients to enter their contact data for an opportunity to win a free excursion.

12. Coupons and arrangements

Extraordinary arrangements can assist you with catching clients at the lower part of the advertising channel — individuals who are choosing whether or not to buy your item. Bargains work in two ways: First, they make a need to keep moving and urge clients to act rapidly before the arrangement is finished. Second, they assist clients with setting aside cash and feel like they're getting an exceptional yield on their speculation.

The sorts of arrangements you can offer are perpetual. Here are a few models:

- Extraordinary introduction offers for first-time clients

- Packaging items together and offering them at a rebate (for instance, a 10-bunch of socks)

- Get one, get one free arrangements

- Refunds

- Occasional deals and limits (like the huge shopping day after Thanksgiving advancements)

- Limits on unique thing classifications

- Birthday coupons for clients

- Free delivery for clients who spend over a specific sum

Best practices for a fruitful advancement technique

Indeed, even the most creative advancement techniques can come up short on the off chance that they're not executed accurately. This is the way to get yours in a good position:

- **Keep advancements basic:** The best advancements techniques are straightforward and simple for clients to comprehend. You would rather not put forth them spend a ton of attempt sorting out what a promotion means or how to recover an arrangement. All things being equal, advancements ought to feel practically easy — so clients don't surrender and choose to spend their cash elsewhere. For instance, keep deals advancement messages basic and direct.

Rather than jumbling the page with text, feature the arrangement and incorporate a source of inspiration button so clients can navigate and reclaim straightforwardly.

• **Measure results and be prepared to change your system:** Not all advancements fill in true to form. That implies it's essential to regularly follow measurements and measure how your technique is performing — for instance, with A/B tests or split tests. This assists you with abstaining from throwing away life on advertising endeavors that aren't working any longer, and immediately adjust when the market climate changes.

• **Restock your item and landing page for advancements:** Individuals become accustomed to seeing your landing page and item a specific way. Re-marketing implies stirring up your innovative technique and changing the look and feel of your landing page or item point of arrival to catch clients' eye. For instance, an online business could add new visual components to their landing page to cause to notice advancements.

- **Make an unmistakable brand:** There are a ton of items on the lookout, so odds are good that you really want to vie for your crowd's consideration. That implies it's vital to zero in on brand separation — exhibiting how your image is superior to the opposition, and what you can offer that different organizations can't. For instance, the staple chain Entire Food varieties put their image aside by elevating a better way to deal with eating and living — in addition to making an outwardly engaging shopping experience.

- **Give a decent client experience:** Your advancement procedure isn't over once clients make a buy. Rather than simply zeroing in on drawing in new clients, ensure existing clients have a decent encounter and need to return to your image later on. Make a client venture guide to plot individuals' thought process, act, and feel all through the purchasing system — then see what upgrades you can make. This could incorporate better client support, a more consistent checkout interaction, or even invite messages and progressing correspondences to keep up with client connections over the long run.

To run an effective advancement methodology, you really want to organize work with various partners. Keep undertakings coordinated with a promoting methodology layout, which can assist you with arranging objectives, distribute assets, and explain technique proprietors — across the board place.

CHAPTER 7:

Leadership and Teamwork

Have you at any point thought about how the most extraordinary organizations and associations in the market figure out how to accomplish their objectives? Collaboration and administration are two fundamental abilities for doing precisely that.

For what reason are collaboration and administration significant for profession achievement?

Collaboration and administration are two of the most valued delicate abilities at organizations today. In particular, collaboration is viewed as key to the development of any task or thought. The capacity to help out others to accomplish targets is an unquestionable necessity, yet to do that effectively requires solid administration who can distinguish the qualities and shortcomings of each and every individual from the group, relegating them reasonable undertakings they can finish on time.

The significance of powerful collaboration and authority lies in the accompanying advantages:

- **Animating innovativeness.** Working in a group builds individuals' imaginative limits since openness to varying perspectives widens skylines and opens new points of view. Besides, when an individual fills in as a feature of a group, they investigate their abilities to the most extreme, with the outcomes being a combination of different ability, which works with the venture's prosperity.

- **Expanded inspiration.** The way that everybody deals with the areas they are generally talented at and prepared to do emphatically affects their inspiration, as well as that of the remainder of the colleagues.

- **Improvement and stream of interchanges.** Playing out this sort of work includes the ideal administration of your relational abilities, such that helps the undertaking and guarantees its fruitful finishing.

- **Expanded efficiency.** Joining various perspectives makes more powerful arrangements. Furthermore, working in a group increments viability, since task finish is not generally kept down by the issues one individual might confront, whether because of absence of time, abilities, and so on. All things being equal, the undertaking can push ahead because of a typical concentration.

- **Better work environment air.** Working in a group assists with making compatibility, by sharing targets and objectives. This prepares for a decent work environment climate, despite the fact that it's significant for any potential struggle that emerges to be managed quickly through reasonable overall vibes. This will keep it from raising further.

- **A superior feeling of having a place.** Functioning collectively, shared accomplishments give an extraordinary feeling of individual fulfillment, which greatly affects the feeling of having a place with the gathering. Far and away superior, this converts into an expansion in inspiration and efficiency.

Key elements for effective collaboration and authority

An organization or association's prosperity is down to how proficiently their groups work. Accomplishing such proficiency is an endless errand that group chiefs need to bear, observing a couple of explicit rules:

1. Great correspondence

Correspondence is the premise of any relationship, and in the realm of work, there must be transparent interchanges between each individual from the gathering. There are numerous ways of empowering correspondence inside an organization. One of these is through gatherings or video meetings in which each colleague advances their interests, sentiments and evaluation of the work being finished.

2. Shared objectives

Collaboration and administration achievement relies upon characterizing and laying out specific objectives that each part is quick to accomplish, satisfying their obligations to do as such.

3. Group direction

It's essential to include colleagues in conceptualizing so that, by considering everybody's perspective, the most fitting procedures can be embraced for the association's advantage. Along these lines, the gatherings develop and advance.

4. Cultivating an environment of trust

Trust is likewise basic with regards to associations between colleagues. Trust is procured and fabricated dynamically, and whenever it's accomplished, individuals will work in an ideal way, taking on liabilities and deliberately supporting the group.

5. Praising triumphs

Who could do without to praise the successes and great outcomes? Doing so helps group inspiration. A decent pioneer values an incredible piece of handiwork and compliments the entire group, as well as every part independently.

Viable cooperation and initiative is vital to any project's prosperity since it assists with streamlining the capacities of each colleague, while likewise cultivating their innovativeness. Besides, this expansion in inspiration significantly affects helping efficiency. So, cooperation enjoys many benefits and applying it to the business climate can demonstrate exceptionally powerful.

Eventually, collaboration and authority are essential for individuals to advance, conquer the difficulties presented by the fourth modern unrest and fill in a comprehensive and feasible manner.

Motivating and Teaming up with Others

Where does joint effort come from? It comes from correspondence, from drive, and from a common energy to accomplish incredible things as an association. Microsoft Office 365 has created this supportive webcast to assist you with understanding how you can cultivate a culture of joint effort in your working environment.

You can put every one of the physical and advanced procedures you like set up however without a basic ethos of coordinated effort, the impact on your work environment will be negligible.

All things being equal, the right climate should be cultivated to hatch cooperation in your office and then some, enveloping your entire association.

Obviously, building cooperatively engaged office spaces and having the apparatuses set up to cooperate on remote undertakings is significant. Yet, this just gives one-half of the arrangement. What you are expecting to accomplish is a social shift; a change in the actual texture of what is most important to your office.

On the off chance that you need cooperation and the benefits it brings, you really want to rouse it. This is the way...

Spread the word

The incentive administration similarity has for some time been taken care of and excused as excessively shortsighted. All things being equal, a more refined - and, yet, blindingly self-evident - approach is required, which is just to frame the benefits of top notch cooperative work.

The inspirations of your colleagues are excessively far reaching and different for a catch-all prizes conspire. For instance, individual staff individuals might have a perplexing arrangement of driving variables in their minds when they approach work.

This implies, what might rouse a portion of your group might be trivial to other people. All things considered, we really want to show the way that joint effort should be possible appropriately and how we can accomplish a serious advantage by taking on this methodology at work.

Examine best practices, inspect contextual investigations, open up a discourse across the entire group, and fabricate the groundworks of a cooperative climate.

The Force of Account

Stories, by their actual nature, are moving. Stories are likewise comprehensive and cooperative. While, these days, we have the possibility of an individual perusing a book alone, presumably a book composed by a solitary individual, this isn't where stories came from.

Stories started with the oral practice; ditties and adventures created cooperatively after some time and conveyed to a group of people altogether. Tap into this thought with regards to moving your group to work cooperatively.

Share stories and encounters. Give an open gathering to others to share their own. By working along these lines, you are assisting with making an environment of activity and sharing, as opposed to detachment and reservation.

While framing the advantages of cooperative work regarding both individual and hierarchical turn of events, construct and delineate areas of strength for a.

Lead From the Front

It's implied that rousing an adjustment of the work environment includes starting to lead the pack and demonstrating the way that it very well may be finished. Obviously, the equivalent is valid for building a cooperation culture. Nonetheless, you might be shocked by the number of pioneers 'talk the discussion' yet neglect to 'walk the stroll' in such manner.

Essentially let your group know what they need to do won't cut it. They as of now comprehend what joint effort is and what cooperation resembles. It depends on you to show them its particular applications inside your association.

Analyze past drives and comprehend how they could be dealt with better from here on out. Consider how groups can be assembled so they are comprised of people who supplement the ranges of abilities of each other. Put yourself on the cutting edge for instance. This is a huge step towards making a cooperative air with a long heritage.

Center around Versatility

Setting the ball moving on cooperation at work requires a level of exertion. This, in any case, isn't the most troublesome aspect of encouraging the right environment.

Getting colleagues familiar with talking about issues and cooperating on various tasks is clear, gave this development is parallel, occurring on a similar bar of the so-called stepping stool.

It gets somewhat more troublesome when in an upward direction coordinated joint effort is required; when versatility between various levels is normal.

This is completely subject to the way of life examined previously. The cutting edge work environment should be the favorable place for a culture of common regard, transparency, and an eagerness to share thoughts.

All colleagues, at all levels, need to feel good and certain that they will be treated with deference at work and that their thoughts will be paid attention to. The flipside of this is that all thoughts - regardless of which echelon of the association the thought comes from - are available to discuss and contemplated conflict.

By making this kind of open and versatile climate, you are making room for advancement. The most shrewd thoughts don't be guaranteed to start at the top however are created cooperatively.
Fabricate Your Tool compartment, and Your Current circumstance

Fostering a positive climate of cooperation is one thing yet this should be upheld by the climate. Your group needs to have a work area where their cooperative endeavors are praised and improved, for instance, through the arrangement of in-house meeting regions and rooms, or by means of equipment pieces intended to empower far off correspondence.

Your group likewise needs a scope of computerized devices, applications and stages to assist them with accomplishing the goals they set for themselves.

These incorporate planning devices to unite errands and to guarantee progress towards put forth objectives, cooperative work stages to bind together endeavors and guarantee everybody is pulling in a similar heading, and computerized frameworks which can deal with a portion of the truly difficult work related with cooperative working, leaving groups allowed to zero in on areas of strength for them.

Motivating shrewd coordinated effort is tied in with laying the basis and ensuring that all components - whether they are physical, computerized, or calculated - are set up. From here, excellent coordinated effort can be effectively accomplished.

Microsoft Office 365 has even created this supportive webcast to assist you with understanding how you can encourage a culture of coordinated effort in your work environment.

CHAPTER 8:

Problem-Solving Skills

Everyone can profit from having great critical thinking abilities as we as a whole experience issues consistently. A portion of these issues are clearly more serious or complex than others.

It would be magnificent to can tackle all issues productively and in an opportune style easily, tragically however there is nobody manner by which all issues can be settled.

Relational connections fall flat and organizations come up short due to unfortunate critical thinking.

This is frequently due to either issues not being perceived or being perceived however not being managed suitably.

Critical thinking abilities are exceptionally pursued by managers as many organizations depend on their workers to distinguish and take care of issues.

A ton of the figure out in critical thinking includes understanding what the basic issues of the issue truly are - not the side effects. Managing a client protest might be viewed as need might arise to be settled, and it's more than likely smart to do as such. The representative managing the protest ought to ask what has made the client gripe in any case, in the event that the reason for the grievance can be dispensed with then the issue is addressed.

To be successful at critical thinking you are probably going to require a few other key abilities, which include:

Inventiveness. Issues are typically addressed either instinctively or efficiently. Instinct is utilized when no new information is required - you realize that enough will generally have the option to pursue a speedy choice and tackle the issue, or you utilize sound judgment or experience to take care of the issue. More complicated issues or issues that you have not experienced before will probably require a more methodical and sensible way to deal with tackle, and for these you should utilize imaginative reasoning. See our page on Imaginative Reasoning for more data.

Investigating Abilities. Characterizing and tackling issues frequently expects you to do some examination: this might be a basic Google search or a more thorough exploration project. See our Exploration Strategies segment for thoughts on the most proficient method to direct powerful examination.

Group Working. Numerous issues are best characterized and settled with the contribution of others. Group working might seem like a 'work thing' yet it is similarly as significant at home and school as well as in the work environment. See our Group Working page for more.
the capacity for profound appreciation of people. It merits thinking about the effect that an issue as

187

well as its answer has on you and others. The capacity to understand people on a deeper level, the capacity to perceive the feelings of yourself as well as other people, will assist with directing you to a proper arrangement. See our Capacity to appreciate people on a deeper level pages for more.

Risk The executives. Tackling an issue implies a specific measure of chance - this hazard should be weighed facing not taking care of the issue. You might find our Gamble The executives page valuable.

Navigation. Critical thinking and navigation are firmly related abilities, and settling on a choice is a significant contributor to the critical thinking process as you will frequently be confronted with different choices and options. See Decision Making for more.

Handling Difficulties with Imagination

Tackling a working environment challenge frequently requires inventive thoughts. Also, in a perfect world you and your group concoct heaps of them. In any case, a couple of will endure to execution and the stunt is recognizing which are the managers and which to give up.

Here are his five hints to assist you with choosing the smartest plans to take forward:

1. Need for speed

A speedy success is something little and clear to do that is a no-second thoughts activity. You would rather not focus on fast wins, you need to zero in on Win Quicklys. These are thoughts that can be executed quickly and that will test, or demonstrate, an intriguing part of something with more prominent potential.

Little Win Quicklies can frequently be more important for your vocation than greater thoughts on the grounds that (a) they assist with limiting gamble for the group executing it, and (b) assist you with getting results sooner. Numerous associations like to perceive how a Success Rapidly demonstrates that something a lot bigger has the potential for progress and worth.

2. Enter the Lattice

A Success Rapidly lattice can assist you with contrasting thoughts and distinguish the ones with progress. This in pairs network estimates how simple a thought is to follow through on the level hub and how well the thought will demonstrate something on the upward pivot. Thoughts that are difficult to do and have a low capacity as evidence focuses will be in the lower-left quadrant, while those that are not difficult to execute and will promptly demonstrate something are in the upper right quadrant.

To start, place one of your thoughts at the focal point of the lattice, and afterward analyze the place of the others as you add them comparative with this first thought. Add around ten thoughts onto the framework, which should all be moderately speedy to convey.

Thoughts in the upper right quadrant that have a high effect and are not difficult to do are the ones that will most allure. In any case, thoughts that have high effect and are difficult to do (the upper left quadrant) may likewise merit considering. Thoughts in the lower half of the grid will have lower influence, so you probably shouldn't consider these by any stretch of the imagination.

3. Squander not need not

There will be thoughts that are considered not sufficient to be on your Success Rapidly network. These thoughts, along with the thoughts you put on the lower half of the lattice, may in any case have an incentive for you. While these thoughts may not be sufficiently able to remain on their own in their ongoing structure, in the event that you join a few of them together (maybe re-molding them), there might be esteem in them you hadn't seen before. Maybe a few distinct thoughts can consolidate and coordinate to become something considerably more intriguing. Or on the other hand perhaps uniting two thoughts ignites a totally groundbreaking thought.

Now and again conveying a few thoughts to you simultaneously is troublesome. A valuable activity to assist you with coordinating thoughts is to compose every one on a tacky note and afterward pair them up in various ways to see what novel insights are set off by each particular mix of stickies. In the event that you want to compose additional stickies to bring in with the general mish-mash, then, at that point, do whatever assists you with your reasoning. It's never past the point of no return for additional groundbreaking thoughts that increase the value of address your large issue.

4. Not about you

It's memorable's vital that regardless of how satisfied you are with your thoughts, you've just tended to it from one perspective - yours. Different perspectives might contrast from yours, and you want to consider whether your proposed arrangement ought to consolidate these varying viewpoints. In this way, take your thoughts for a test drive to see others' thought process of them - they might have insight and information to assist you with expanding on your thoughts.

The point is to design your thoughts into rich and even minded arrangements, and others can assist with this. Continuously think about an expected arrangement as a work underway at this stage, and not as a live with or without it thought. Be available to being explained why your thought might be hard to try yet request ways of defeating the issue being raised, and afterward consolidate those ideas.

5. Selling adaptable arrangements

Recollect that a senior individual is probably going to have more information than you of exercises in progress in your association that your proposition needs to line up with. So be adaptable. Sell your proposition as a versatile arrangement they can support, shape, and advantage from. Make sense of how you've connected with others in your reasoning, as this helps show you as a cooperative person and how your reasoning has been approved by significant individuals.

Present your idea as one that can be coordinated and molded - how it gets altered as it advances is irrelevant. You can't be aware or control these components, notwithstanding, it's as yet your thought being examined - and at last carried out.

Utilizing visuals and words that empower various translations through equivocalness can be useful. Essentially, you can offer a scope of choices for any answer for support substitute contemplating how your idea could at last look. Permitting partners to recommend changes, or ways of carrying out it, shows interest from them, and assists you with acquiring purchase in for your proposition.

Reward tip: Charming thoughts

You might have a couple of thoughts that aren't Win Quicklies, and which you haven't advanced at this point since they aren't sufficient. Be that as it may, your psyche won't relinquish them for reasons unknown.

This is your instinct kicking in around some captivating part of these thoughts. You may not know why this is right now, so stand by. Record them on paper and allow them to hatch to you. Since they interest you, your psyche won't let them go, and when you return to them in half a month's time, don't be shocked in the event that a few new experiences come out immediately.

CHAPTER 9:

Financial Success

Is it true or not that you are searching for ways of making monetary progress however feel overpowered with how much exhortation accessible? Monetary achievement is reachable for everybody with the right propensities and methodologies. It's essential to lay out a monetary arrangement that permits you to monitor your headway and to make changes depending on the situation. Having great cash the board abilities is vital to monetary achievement. Creating propensities that will assist you with arriving at your monetary objectives is fundamental. In this blog entry, we will examine the main ten propensities to assist you with making monetary progress. We will examine the significance of planning, saving, money management, and that's only the tip of the iceberg. By integrating these propensities into your day to day daily practice, you will end up on the way to monetary achievement. Peruse on to find the main ten propensities that will assist you with capitalizing on your cash and make monetary progress.

1. Track your spending and adhere to a financial plan

Perhaps of the main propensity you can take on to guarantee your monetary prosperity is to follow your spending and adhere to a financial plan. Laying out a financial plan and following your spending assists you with remaining in charge of your funds and guarantee that you are not overspending. Monitoring where your cash is going permits you to recognize regions where you might have the option to save or regions where you can decrease your spending. Monetary achievement is tied in with making sure you are spending your cash carefully and planning really is an extraordinary method for doing that.

2. Live beneath your means

One of the vital standards for making monetary progress is to live underneath your means. This implies that you ought to abstain from overspending and on second thought center around setting aside and putting away your cash. By setting a financial plan and adhering to it, you can guarantee that you are just spending what you want and involving the remainder of your pay for

reserve funds and speculations. This will furnish you with a strong starting point for monetary prosperity and monetary achievement.

3. Put resources into yourself and your profession

Number three on our rundown of propensities for making monetary progress is to put resources into yourself and your profession. Putting resources into yourself is tied in with ensuring you have what it takes, information and experience that will set you in a situation to bring in additional cash and increment your monetary prosperity. This could mean taking courses to improve your expert turn of events, organizing in the business you might want to work in, or exploring different jobs that could bring about really acquiring potential. Moreover, putting resources into your vocation could mean devoting time to making a portfolio, joining proficient associations, and going to gatherings and workshops. By finding opportunity to put resources into yourself and your vocation, you'll have the option to make the most of additional open doors that could work on your monetary achievement.

4. Computerize your reserve funds

Computerizing your reserve funds is a fundamental propensity to assist with making monetary progress. Computerizing your reserve funds assists with guaranteeing your record balance is developing in any event, when you're not effectively mulling over everything. By setting up a mechanized exchange or direct store from your check into an investment account, retirement record, or speculations, you'll have the option to set aside cash without mulling over everything. This can assist you with arriving at your monetary objectives quicker and accomplish monetary prosperity. Mechanizing your investment funds is a simple method for ensuring effective monetary administration.

5. Influence build interest

Fifth on the rundown of propensities to assist with making monetary progress is to use build interest. Build interest is a distinct advantage in the weapons store of any serious abundance manufacturer. It works by permitting cash to procure revenue on the past premium acquired. It is an integral asset that, when utilized carefully, can assist you with developing your abundance dramatically after some time. For instance, assuming you put $1,000 in a bank account that offers 5% yearly premium, following 10 years, you would have procured $1,500 in revenue alone. That is a half profit from your unique speculation. Monetary achievement is reachable when you utilize build interest for your potential benefit.

6. Limit obligation

Limiting obligation is indispensable for making monetary progress, and is vital to keeping up with monetary prosperity. Charge card obligation, understudy loans, and different kinds of obligation can rapidly add up, and can become overpowering in the event that not oversaw as expected. Focusing on obligation reimbursement and paying off your obligation burden can assist with making inward feeling of harmony and monetary security. Begin by making a financial plan and designating your assets to obligation reimbursement. Consider using balance move Visas or applying for a line of credit with a lower loan cost to combine your obligation. At long last, form a secret stash to assist with guaranteeing you can take care of any startling costs.

7. Research speculations and grasp risk

Monetary achievement requires informed choices. Prior to money management reserves, it is important to comprehend the gamble related with the speculation. Exploring ventures should be possible through perusing monetary distributions and counseling monetary guides. Understanding the gamble related with speculations will prompt more educated choices and better monetary prosperity.

8. Use tax reductions:

Exploiting tax cuts can be a significant calculate making monetary progress. Tax cuts can be as derivations, credits, and different exclusions that bring down your available pay and, in this way, decrease how much duties owed. Try to investigate as needs be and talk with a certified duty expert to guarantee that you are making the most of the tax cuts accessible to you and your loved ones. Doing so can set aside you cash and assist you with accomplishing monetary prosperity.

9. Save for retirement

Retirement arranging is a significant piece of accomplishing monetary prosperity and monetary achievement. To have a protected retirement, it is vital for begin saving early and reliably. A decent guideline is to save 15% of your pay every month. You ought to likewise think about putting resources into stocks and bonds, as well as some other retirement vehicles that might be accessible in your space. Moreover, it is vital to monitor your retirement commitments and guarantee that they are developing every year. With legitimate preparation, you can guarantee that you have an agreeable retirement when the opportunity arrives.

10. Foster various floods of pay

Fostering numerous surges of pay is a significant propensity to assist with making monetary progress. Having more than one kind of revenue gives you more monetary strength. It likewise gives you more command over your monetary prosperity. Whether you're keen on beginning a side gig, turning into a financial backer, or building a business, having various surges of pay will assist you with creating financial momentum over the long haul. It's essential to expand your types of revenue, so you're not depending on only one to keep you above water.

Monetary achievement can be accomplished by developing the right propensities. Propensities like planning, following costs, defining monetary objectives, and contributing for the future are fundamental for building serious areas of strength for an establishment. While it might require an investment and work to lay out sure monetary propensities, the outcomes are certainly worth the work. With the right propensities set up, you should rest assured to make monetary progress.

Dealing with Your Cash as long as possible

What is cash the board?
Planning, financial planning, saving and in any event, burning through are each of the a piece of cash the executives. So how would you construct cash certainty and diminish nervousness about your monetary objectives? Tracking down ways of bettering deal with your cash — and your outlook — could help. You could do your own

exploration or get proficient guidance to help you with your monetary arrangement.

The most effective method to deal with your cash better

You could utilize these seven functional monetary tips and cash the board abilities as a general aide for your monetary excursion.

1. Make an individual spending plan

Individuals feeling the effects of monetary pressure battle more with planning — that is one finding from the Capital One Brain Over Cash study. They feel less in charge and will generally spend their checks all the more imprudently.

Making a financial plan is an extraordinary initial phase in creating better cash propensities and figuring out how to maximize your cash.

As indicated by the Buyer Monetary Security Department (CFPB), "planning guarantees that you'll have sufficient cash for the things you want and the things you need, while as yet fabricating your reserve funds for future objectives."

You could begin by utilizing a planning worksheet and following general advances like these:

- **Include your month to month pay.** This incorporates your compensation at your particular employment in addition to different kinds of revenue like rewards, charge discounts or pay from side work.

- **Include your month to month expenses.** These can remember costs for the major "pails" like covering bills for lodging, food, understudy loans and transportation. For regularly scheduled installments that aren't generally something very similar — food and utilities, for instance — you could utilize a normal from earlier months.

- **Deduct your costs from your pay.** This sum will be the beginning spot for your financial plan. Anything left over is what you need to work with while you're squaring away obligation and developing investment funds.

On the off chance that what's left is excessively little, you might need to consider reducing expenses for things like takeout food and memberships, in the event that you haven't as of now.

It might assist with considering your spending plan a living report that you take a gander at frequently. Like that, you can make changes assuming that you really want to, similar to when you take out a month to month cost by taking care of a Visa. You could likewise consider famous planning draws near, similar to the 50/30/20 rule, while making your spending plan.

2. Track your spending

The Capital One Brain Over Cash investigation discovered that utilizing solid cash propensities when you have good expectations about your funds can help you when things get seriously testing.

One of those healthy habits could be keeping track of your expenditures. All things considered, it might assist you with trying not to overspend and remain affordable enough for you.

How would you monitor your spending? It's straightforward. You could record your costs carefully with one of the various applications accessible on the web.

Assuming that you have a Capital One card, you could utilize the free computerized highlights that assist you with following your cash. Or on the other hand, in the event that you favor a paper-based choice, you could basically save your receipts and track everything in an organizer or journal.

Here's a hint for one how-to: You may need to separate your expenses into classes. Like that, you'll see precisely where your cash is going and where you might spend excessively.

3. Save for retirement

The Capital One Psyche Over Cash investigation found that Americans are anxious about their financial future, as one might expect. That incorporates putting something aside for retirement. As a matter of fact, 68% of respondents said they're stressed they will not have sufficient cash to resign.

It might assist with beginning little with regards to retirement investment funds. As such, you could save a limited quantity consistently for the time being, and afterward add to it when you feel prepared.

It might likewise assist with opening a retirement plan account that could enhance retirement pay from benefits or Federal retirement aide. These kinds of records might incorporate the accompanying:

- **401(k) plan through your manager.** With a 401(k), you can store pretax dollars through an ordinary derivation from your check. Beth Sabin, a leader at Capital One, says, "Assuming you have an organization match through your 401(k), this can be an extraordinary spot to begin by contributing until you have your full match." She likewise suggests increasing your commitment by 1 rate highlight check whether that is feasible for you. On the off chance that it is, you could increment it by another rate highlight speed up your reserve funds.

- **403(b) plan.** Like 401(k) plans, 403(b) plans are manager supported. One distinction is that 403(b) plans are presented by state funded schools and a few associations that are charge excluded. Commitments to customary 403(b) plans are charge conceded — very much like they are with conventional 401(k) plans. So you don't need to pay charges on the commitments or profit until you pull out assets from the record.

- **Individual retirement account (IRA).** Commitments to a customary IRA — a record that is by and large independently managed and not supported by a business — are charge conceded. When you resign and begin making withdrawals, the cash will be charged at your normal annual expense rate.

- **Roth IRA.** While commitments to a Roth IRA aren't charge deductible when you make them, you might have the option to pull out your cash tax exempt during your retirement years.

However, you might need to counsel your duty guide for more data about these plans.

Remember that progressive accrual can be a significant motivation to ambitious beginning saving. As the CFPB makes sense of, accumulate revenue might assist you with speeding up your investment funds by acquiring revenue on premium. To perceive how accumulated dividends can add up, you might need to attempt this Accruing funds Number cruncher from the U.S. Protections and Trade Commission.

4. Save for crises

Taking care of investment funds in a rainy day account for surprising life altering situations — like requiring significant home fixes — may assist you with resting easier thinking about your monetary circumstance.

Developing your investment funds may be one of your objectives. On the off chance that it is, you might need to consider these money tips to assist with unforeseen costs:

- **Keep in mind, financing costs can differ.** So it could be savvy to look around. On the off chance that you find an investment account with a superior rate, the additional premium can accumulate over the long haul.

. Put additional pay into your record. At the point when you get an expense discount or a reward at your particular employment, consider saving it into your financial balance. The additional cash can assist your investment funds with developing.

- **Purchase what you really want as opposed to what you need.** Like that, you can put the rest toward your reserve funds.

- **Set up programmed investment funds.** With the assistance of your boss, you might have the option to set up programmed moves to your bank account to fabricate your investment funds without the allurement of expenditure additional money.

5. Plan to take care of obligation

Taking care of obligation may likewise assist you with better dealing with your funds and lessen cash related tension.

The CFPB has recommended the following two plans for becoming obligation-free:

- **Snowball technique:** This strategy centers around taking care of your littlest equilibriums first. You actually make the base installments on your obligations as a whole. At the same time, you use any extra money to pay for your smallest balance. Then you utilize the cash you've opened up to take care of your next-littlest equilibrium, etc. This could mean obligations with higher financing costs could end up taking more time to pay off. Also, that could set you back more over the long haul.

- **Obligation torrential slide technique:** In this strategy — additionally called the most elevated loan fee strategy — you list your obligations in light of their financing costs, from most noteworthy to least. Your funds are applied to the debt that has the highest interest rate first. Whenever that is paid off, those additional assets can be utilized to take care of the following credit on your rundown. In addition, you continue to fulfill all of your obligations by making the minimum payments.

6. Lay out great credit propensities
Pursuing laying out great FICO assessments could likewise assist with working on your funds.

As per the CFPB, your FICO ratings are a depiction of your financial soundness. So these scores can influence many pieces of your life —

all that from leasing a loft to being considered for a task.

The CFPB suggests the accompanying as a feature of an individual budget the executives intend to construct great credit:

- Cover your bills on time — every single month.

- Try not to draw near as far as possible on your credit accounts.
- Work at laying out a long record as a consumer.

Routinely checking your credit reports for exactness might help as well. CreditWise from Capital One is a simple method for checking your VantageScore® 3.0 financial assessment and TransUnion® credit report. It won't hurt your FICO assessments. Furthermore, it's free for everybody, regardless of whether you have a Capital One item. You can likewise get free duplicates of your credit reports from every one of the three significant credit authorities at AnnualCreditReport.com.

As you make progress toward your monetary objectives, you could likewise look at how as a Capital One Visa fits in. With mindful use, you could utilize one to fabricate or revamp your credit on your monetary excursion.

7. Further develop your cash outlook

How you manage your cash is significant. In any case, your opinion on it tends to be significant as well.

Developing a more confident financial mindset when managing money may involve maintaining focus on your goals. It might also entail taking an answer-focused approach and focusing on the areas where you have some control, such as paying back debt and handling finances.

For more about these and other individual cash the board tips for a superior cash mentality, look at the Capital One Psyche Over Cash study.

Keep in mind, you're in good company assuming you're having a focused on outlook on the best way to oversee cash, handle individual accounting records or hit your reserve funds objectives. Be that as it may, presently you find out about techniques for dealing with your cash, setting your month to month spending plan, reimbursing obligations and building your secret stash. Assuming you continue to work at them, they may ultimately become propensities. Also, that could end up being useful to set you up for monetary accomplishment at each phase of your life.

CHAPTER 10:

Work-Life Equilibrium

Feeling like all you do is work?

You're in good company. A few insights show that in excess of 60% of U.S. representatives feel like their balance between serious and fun activities is messed up. Be that as it may, how would you adjust your work-existence with such a lot of work occurring at home? Also, how would you adjust your responsibility to be more proficient?

Is it something beyond hitting a week by week yoga class? Furthermore, in particular, in reality as we know it where the limits among work and home are progressively obscured, how would you sort out what functions?

With so many battling to secure congruity between their positions and their home life, it can appear to be unavoidable to feel overpowered and exhausted. In any case, it doesn't need to be.

Here I have distinguished the designing of sound and unfortunate balance between fun and serious activities and ways people and administrators can track down better approaches to overseeing both.

What takes care of business life balance mean?

Solid balance between serious and fun activities alludes to keeping an amicable connection between your work and individual life. It includes intentionally dealing with your significant investment to meet both expert and individual responsibilities while focusing on taking care of oneself and prosperity.

In an ideal world, this thought process goes: after work, we're ready to invest energy on things that feed us as individuals. This could include investing energy with loved ones or taking part in a leisure activity.

Several characteristics of a well-balanced mix of serious and enjoyable activities could be:

- **Defining limits:** This includes laying out clear limits among work and individual life by characterizing explicit working hours and isolating business related assignments from individual exercises.

- **Using time effectively:** Proficiently putting together and focusing on undertakings, guaranteeing that you designate sufficient time for work liabilities as well as special goals, like investing energy with family, taking part in leisure activities, or seeking after private objectives

- **Stress the executives:** Carrying out systems to oversee feelings of anxiety, for example, rehearsing care, participating in ordinary actual work, enjoying reprieves,

and turning off from business related
exercises when required

- **Adaptability:** Being able to adjust and
  change your timetable to oblige
  unanticipated conditions or individual
  requirements without risking work
  responsibilities

Why is balance between fun and serious activities so significant?

Very much like in our eating regimens, to remain
sound and stimulated for the long stretch,
individuals need assortment. With regards to
balance between fun and serious activities,
individuals need to participate in various
exercises and rest. We will generally fall into the
snare of accepting that we can be useful
constantly, or that an eight-hour day at work
compares to eight hours of result. Nonetheless,
that is hard, in the event that certainly feasible,
for some people to accomplish.

In addition, exhausting has adverse results for the two workers and managers.

Compulsive workers and the individuals who battle to rehearse taking care of oneself wind up at higher gamble for burnout, exhaustion, and stress-related medical problems. Unfortunate balance between fun and serious activities can likewise leave representatives working more hours however being less useful.

What is an undesirable balance between fun and serious activities?

Then again, an undesirable balance between fun and serious activities happens when work becomes overpowering and overshadows individual life, prompting unfortunate results for a singular's prosperity. A few indications of an unfortunate balance between fun and serious activities might include:

- **Steady exhaust:** Consistently working extended periods, including ends of the week and occasions, without adequate time for rest, unwinding, or individual exercises

- **Disregarded individual life:** Forfeiting individual connections, side interests, and relaxation exercises because of unreasonable work requests

Keep in mind, accomplishing a sound balance between serious and fun activities might fluctuate from one individual to another, contingent upon individual conditions and inclinations. Essential to find an equilibrium works for yourself and advances your general prosperity.

Indications of an unequal work-life dynamic

Unfortunate balance between serious and fun activities can have a far greater effect than simply skirting the rec center. One investigation discovered that the gamble of stroke is higher in individuals that work over 55 hours per week. Similar measure of work hours is likewise connected with a higher gamble of uneasiness and misery. Furthermore, in any event, while adapting to genuinely ordinary rest designs, one more investigation discovered that functioning longer hours corresponded with a decrease in actual wellbeing.

By its actual definition, balance between serious and fun activities influences all parts of your life. It will in general show up distinctively for various individuals, be that as it may. The following are eight attributes related with unfortunate equilibrium:

- **You can't quit contemplating work when you're not working.** The individuals who find it hard to draw limits among work and life are at higher gamble of burnout.

- **Your connections** — both inside and beyond work — are starting to endure. You might be effectively disturbed with collaborators and far off with friends and family.

- **You feel off.** You have unexplained a throbbing painfulness. You may seldom have energy or find it hard to concentrate when at work.

- **At the point when you're not working, everything appears to be tedious or insignificant.** You simply don't want to do anything except if you need to. You frequently turn down solicitations, further disconnecting yourself from your companions.

- **You burn through huge amount of cash reevaluating support for individual assignments.** Your clothing, dishes, and mail stack up, sitting tight for the day when "have the opportunity" to find time for them.

- **You battle to get some much needed rest when you're wiped out, intellectually stressed, or when you want to deal with individual undertakings.** You don't recall your last get-away and you don't have plans to take one.

- **You can't envision doing how you help the remainder of your life.** Regardless of whether you work in a field or an organization you once cherished, it feels difficult to envision proceeding with life all things considered for a really long time.

You generally feel like regardless of what you're doing, you ought to accomplish something different. After some time, this absence of presence and bearing frequently prompts an existential emergency.

Step by step instructions to further develop balance between fun and serious activities

Truly, there's no solution that will fit everybody. Also, you might need to play with what time scale feels generally applicable to you. Attempting to find balance in any single day might feel disappointing, yet the equilibrium might be simpler to accomplish across possibly more than seven days.

The most effective way to decide the best equilibrium for you is by figuring out how to check in with your inward compass — and your outcomes.

With deliberateness and a little imagination, you can recalibrate your assumptions and reset your work-home equilibrium.

The following are 12 hints to have great your balance between fun and serious activities:

1. Prepare

Prepare to consolidate work exercises with recreation, social, or wellness exercises. On the off chance that you end up with a few virtual gatherings one after the other, have a go at taking them while you take a walk. You could likewise accept a call outside (in the event that surrounding clamor permits!) or welcome a companion over to work with you.

2. Embrace the manner in which your mind works

Use efficiency hacks like a Pomodoro clock to work so, engaged explodes. Shut out any remaining interruptions so you can capitalize on your time.

3. Set blocks of time for various errands

Assign an opportunity to check (and answer) messages, a chance to take gatherings, and a chance to accomplish intellectually escalated work. It assists with securing these undertakings around the times that you are actually more useful.

4. End work at a specific time

There's an expression that "work grows to occupy the time distributed," and when you telecommute, it's much more straightforward to allow work to pour out over into individual time. Put down a point in time to end work for the afternoon, and support it by shutting down business related gadgets, locking your office, or planning something subsequently.

5. Enroll innovation to assist you with turning off

Utilize an application to impede diverting sites during the day, and afterward block work apparatuses late night. In the event that you would be able, limit work to one gadget, or attempt to keep one sans work gadget so you can detach totally.

6. Go out for lunch, or appreciate lunch with colleagues

Regardless of whether you're telecommuting, you can go out for your mid-day break or associate with partners. The difference in speed will be reviving — and, obviously, will remind you to eat something as a matter of fact.

7. Go on vacation

At the point when you're home constantly, you will quite often attempt to deal with sicknesses that unquestionably would have kept you home from the workplace. Downtime, including wiped out time, individual time, get-aways, and deprivation, are significant ways of feeding your prosperity.

8. Practice care

Care makes lopsidedness hard to overlook. At the point when you practice care methods, similar to reflection or breath mindfulness, you become more in line with your feelings and actual sensations. Focusing on these sentiments assists you with figuring out how to see when you may be stifling a need to work. It's difficult to get back to that accounting sheet after you notice your stomach thundering.

9. Find something you love beyond work to participate in

Assuming you have something that you're amped up for accomplishing after work, it will make it simpler to disengage from work messages or end your day at a foreordained time. Our side interests support our energy and imperativeness. At the point when we play and feel inventive, we take our new selves back to work.

10. Reexamine work that causes you to long for balance

Assuming your work feels totally inconsequential to the exercises that mix your advantage, excitement, energy, and feeling of importance, you might have to take a gander at how you can change the work you do or the manner in which you make it happen. While work doesn't have to (and can't) fulfill each of your requirements for reason, meaning, social association, and challenge, we can anticipate that work should give snapshots of fulfillment, achievement, and association.

11. Speak with your director

Unfortunate balance between fun and serious activities is much of the time exacerbated by the trepidation that we're not doing what's necessary. Conversing with your chiefs can assist you with focusing on where to invest your energy. On the off chance that there truly is a lot to do, it very well may be an ideal opportunity to discuss employing extra assistance or smoothing out specific undertakings.

12. Work with a mentor or specialist

In the event that you feel overpowered, stuck, or don't have the foggiest idea where to start to separate, working with an expert can be significant. A mentor or instructor can pose the right inquiries and assist you with recognizing which changes will have the greatest effect and how to get everything rolling.

Single word of exhortation: begin little. In spite of the fact that you might be restless for your balance between serious and fun activities to improve, your work propensities have been worked after some time and possible won't change for the time being. If your objective, for instance, is to lessen screen time, attempting to limit yourself to a specific number of hours will most likely disappoint you. You're bound to stay with another propensity in the event that you start with a more modest objective — say, one five-minute sans tech break a day.

7 different ways directors can uphold their representatives' balance between fun and serious activities

Doing whatever it takes to foster a sound balance between fun and serious activities can be troublesome. As a supervisor and a sympathetic pioneer, you can help your workers (and yourself) by building pathways for them to roll out these improvements. The following are seven different ways chiefs can assist their representatives with building great balance between fun and serious activities:

1. Remind your group to turn off

Urge your group to leave their PCs and work telephones at home when they take some time off. You might figure it needn't bother with to be said, yet they will see the value in the unequivocal authorization.

2. Give workers space to interface

Sort out virtual cheerful hours, birthday celebrations, book clubs, and different chances to socially associate. Put your mid-day break on your schedule so they can see that you eat, as well.

3. Instruct workers on their advantages

Remind your workers that debilitated leave and PTO are important for their pay, and remember to exploit them yourself! With regards to going on vacation, talk is cheap.

4. Check in with direct reports

Make time during your registrations to get some information about worker prosperity. You might need to find out a deeper meaning for what's not being said. Missed cutoff times or an absence of responsiveness can show overpower.

5. Set a model for your group

Take gatherings while strolling, acquaint them with your children on Zoom (we definitely know they're there), or space out gatherings so they make them inhale room.

6. Know about organization culture and standards

Make an effort not to standardize an "texting" culture. Clarify that messages sent on off-hours don't need prompt consideration, and stay away from deciphering responsiveness as commitment.

7. Regard working hours

Try not to plan gatherings previously or after work hours. This can be precarious while working across various time regions. Urge your representatives to end work at an assigned time every day, and check in with anybody you notice reliably working late night.

Finding balance between serious and fun activities while working from a distance

One could figure working remotely would make it simpler to accomplish a balance between fun and serious activities. In any case, remote work presents its own difficulties. Working beyond the workplace will in general mean performing various tasks, interruptions, and trouble keeping severe hours — all awful news for efficiency as well as keeping work and life isolated.

Preceding the Covid pandemic, roughly 20% of the U.S. labor force telecommuted. For all intents and purposes for the time being, that number soar to almost 70%. Homes became places for work, school, feasts, recreation, and, surprisingly, working out.

There are a few clear potential gains. It's never been simpler to carry your own lunch to work, busy time is a relic of days gone by, and it just requires a moment to throw in a heap of clothing before your next gathering.

Notwithstanding, captivating in different exercises in a similar space makes it harder for your mind to recognize work and recreation. We come up short on typical prompts of individuals passing on the workplace to flag when the time has come to wrap up work.

When your "office" is a side of your room or your lounge area table, it makes it hard to quit pondering work when work is finished — and simple to browse your email only once again. Furthermore, despite the fact that we recover time from a drive, many individuals miss that reality to change from home life to endlessly work life to home.

In a period of social separating, our balance between serious and fun activities is now battling. For some, our work has generally acclimated to the pandemic, however a significant number of our recreation exercises and most loved outlets have not. Accordingly, it's considerably more straightforward to get maneuvered into work. We might trust that the gathering with the Promoting group will give to some extent a touch of the sought after friendly communication and feeling that we'd typically get at the rec center, a show, or going out with companions.

Find and keep a sound balance between serious and fun activities

Finding that the connection among work and home life is wrong is the most vital phase in correcting it. It could require some investment, yet little everyday or week after week propensities can have a colossal effect over the long haul. In the event that you really want assistance in working out an arrangement to further develop your balance between serious and fun activities, training can help.

Accomplishing a Satisfying Profession and Individual Life

Understanding Time: 3 minutes

With regards to contemplating your profession, you might feel threatened or overpowered. How would you figure out some kind of harmony between pursuing your profession objectives and keeping a significant individual life? Fit all parts of your existence with these tips:

Begin with "why"

Ask yourself, for what reason would you say you are doing this? For what reason would you say you are seeking after this major or profession? Consider everything you are energetic about. Regardless of what your interests might be, associate them to your profession. In doing as such, you promptly put your feeling of satisfaction at the very front of your needs.

Settle on your own meaning of accomplishment

You've most likely adult with different meanings of progress: running the quickest in the track group, scoring the most noteworthy on your numerical test, or getting entrance into an esteemed school. Truly, in the event that you need an opportunity to achieve your goals, you really want to characterize accomplishment according to your very own preferences. You might be fulfilled assuming you make progress that really makes a difference to you. This implies tossing out the impression of others and conjuring a picture of success that impacts you. Be explicit, and don't be apprehensive assuming your fantasies feel too large or excessively intense.

Be vital with your time

Ensure your profession and individual life are at balance by utilizing your time carefully. How? Make an arrangement, record your timetable, and incorporate expected clashes. In doing this, you're bound to finish your objectives since you will have outlined answers for potential issues. Utilize your resolve to take care of your responsibilities, and afterward utilize the remainder of your time for exercises you appreciate. Be particular with where you put your energy. In the event that you are a major slowpoke, look at these ways of focusing on your plan for the day.

Explain your objectives for what's in store

Like characterizing your prosperity, put forth objectives in all aspects of your life. While setting out on an excursion, it means quite a bit to know where you are going! Ensure they are unmistakable and line up with your needs. Objective setting not your solidarity? Here are some places to start.

Hold envy in line

Try not to feel undermined by the progress of others. Comprehend that everybody's process appears to be unique, everybody is on an alternate timetable, and you're not in contest with anybody. Assuming you at any point feel envy crawling once more into your framework, interface back to your own meaning of progress. It probably includes working on yourself with next to no correlation with others. Keep in mind, achievement is certainly not a diminishing asset. Since a companion is fruitful, doesn't mean there is less progress on the planet for you to accomplish. There is a lot to go around!

Push yourself beyond your normal comfort zone.

You don't need to do this constantly, however cause a ruckus periodically. At the point when lost in a tedious everyday practice, you might neglect to live completely in every second. In accomplishing something that alarms you, your life will feel even more energetic as a result of it! Likewise, stay open to the likelihood that your meaning of progress might change over the long haul. Change occurs, and that is fine. Embrace it!

Find opportunity to reflect

Take a gander at your associations with your companions, family, and self. Consider all that you've achieved in the previous year. Ask yourself, in each aspect of your life (socially, expertly, scholastically, sincerely, and so on),

"Do I maintain that the following year of my life should seem as though the final remaining one?"Pay attention to the reaction in your stomach. Make a rundown of your achievements, pause for a minute to see the value in how far you've come, and express gratefulness for everything that has made you the individual you are today.

Recall that satisfaction is found inside

You won't track down never-ending satisfaction in money related achievement, someone else, or large number of Instagram devotees. The sooner you understand that you are the way in to your own satisfaction, the nearer you'll be to finding a balance between serious and fun activities that is ideal for you. Consider this statement from Aeschylus, "Joy is a decision that requires exertion some of the time." It sounds senseless to feel that we can opt for satisfaction when we can't necessarily in every case control our conditions. How would you acknowledge confidence when you are managed a particularly

247

troublesome hand? However there might be times when euphoria feels impossible, you have the ability to take what is going on and transform into a good.

CHAPTER 11:

Adapting to Change

Large numbers of us might wind up inquiring, "How would you adjust to transform?" It's an intricate inquiry. Be that as it may, the rule is to 'change, adjust, and survive.' Regardless of the progressions you're confronting, this article will give pragmatic moves toward assist you with cruising through the excursion all the more easily.

What is flexibility?

Versatility is the capacity to change our considerations, sentiments, and ways of behaving to deal with new, testing, or complex circumstances. A fundamental characteristic empowers people to explore life's progressions and answer successfully to eccentric circumstances.

Here are central issues about flexibility:

- It includes being available to change and embracing it as a chance for development.

- Flexibility is an expertise that can be utilized by different individuals, including experts, understudies, and people confronting individual difficulties.

- It very well may be created and sharpened through training and a consistent learning mentality.

How does versatility function?

Versatility isn't just about enduring change; it's tied in with keeping an uplifting outlook in the midst of it. So how can it function? How does the brain research of adjusting to change assist us with exploring new circumstances?

Flexibility includes the accompanying stages:

Mindfulness

This is where you perceive that a change has happened or is going to occur. Staying alert assists you with grasping the nature and effect of the change on you.

Acknowledgment

This includes finding a sense of peace with the change. Acknowledgment doesn't mean you concur with the change, yet rather that you recognize it's working out and begin working with it as opposed to opposing it.

Learning

Adjusting to change frequently requires acquiring or taking on new abilities. This nvolves being available to new encounters, looking for information, and gaining from others.

Execution

This is where we set our learning up as a regular occurrence. At this stage, you'll see the advantages of your endeavors to adjust, and your trust in managing comparative changes develops.

Advantages of adjusting to change

Adjusting to change can assist us with developing, learn, and lead a really satisfying life and profession. The following are a couple of advantages of adjusting to change:

Decreasing pressure and uneasiness

Change frequently achieves vulnerability, which might prompt uneasiness. Notwithstanding, adjusting to change can assist you with dealing with these feelings. At the point when we embrace transform, we diminish the feeling of dread toward the obscure and, thusly, bring down our pressure and nervousness levels.

Self-improvement

Adjusting to change permits us to learn new things, foster new abilities, and better grasp ourselves and capacities. By venturing beyond our usual ranges of familiarity and embracing change, we cultivate self-awareness and improve our identity worth and certainty.

Upgraded execution

In an expert setting or work environment, adjusting to change can prompt superior execution. Change frequently brings new open doors and conceivable outcomes, and the individuals who adjust successfully are almost certain first to jump all over these chances, prompting professional success and expanded work fulfillment.

Further developed critical thinking

Adjusting to change requires thinking imaginatively and tracking down answers for new difficulties. By improving our critical thinking abilities, we can likewise diminish pressure and uneasiness related with change as we become more prepared to handle and beat impediments.

Upper hand

In the present cutthroat world, flexibility is a vital consider remaining ahead. Enterprises and markets continually develop, and the people who adjust rapidly enjoy a huge benefit. Versatile people and associations can answer market requests successfully, and remain pertinent in evolving patterns, giving them an upper hand.

Step by step instructions to adjust to change

Life has a few changes going from paltry to overpowering and life changing. This implies that the capacity to adjust to change isn't only a convenient expertise yet a crucial life resource.

The following are different procedures, activities, and exercises to assist you with creating versatility in your day to day existence.

Strategies for adjusting to change throughout everyday life and work environment

Strategies assume an imperative part in creating flexibility. Here are a few strategies to consider:

- **Embrace a development outlook:** Take on a mentality that perspectives change as a chance for development and learning. Consider difficulties to be transitory and have confidence in your capacity to adjust and survive.

- **Practice self-reflection:** Carve out opportunity to think about your qualities, objectives, and yearnings. Utilize this change as a chance to survey and realign your way with your valid self.

- **Embrace adaptability:** Challenge unbending idea designs and investigate elective viewpoints. Embrace interest and liberality to cultivate versatility in your reasoning.

Look for help: Going through change alone can overpower. It is crucial for look for help from companions, family, or experts during testing times. By sharing our interests and looking for direction, we can acquire important bits of knowledge, track down consolation, and feel less separated.

Versatility works out

Activities can assist with building up versatility abilities and energize self-improvement. Here are a few activities to upgrade your flexibility:

- **Journaling:** Expound on testing circumstances you have confronted and how you adjusted to them. Ponder what you realized and recognize procedures you can apply from now on.

- **Pretending:** Work on placing yourself in various situations that require flexibility. Investigate alternate points of view and consider elective answers for expand your reasoning.

- **Care and reflection:** Take part in care practices to develop present-second mindfulness and non-critical acknowledgment. This can assist you answer changing conditions with lucidity and serenity.

Versatility exercises

Taking part in unambiguous exercises can additionally foster your versatility abilities. Think about the accompanying exercises:

- **Chipping in:** Take part in humanitarian effort or local area projects that open you to assorted encounters and difficulties. This can extend your point of view and improve your versatility.

- **Acquiring new abilities:** Seek after amazing chances to master new abilities or investigate new areas of premium. Embracing the growing experience and getting out of your usual range of familiarity encourage flexibility.

- **Embracing change:** Search out potential chances to eagerly embrace change. This could incorporate difficult new leisure activities, investigating different social conditions, or taking on new obligations at work or in private life.

Instances of adjusting to change

Here, we'll investigate a few engaging guides to show the way that people can effectively adjust to changes throughout everyday life and working environment.

Instances of adjusting to changes throughout everyday life

Adjusting to changes in life can envelop different situations that shape our self-improvement. These changes, whether expected or unexpected, can affect our lives. Here are a few models:

Vocation change

Emily had been working in similar industry for quite a long time when she out of nowhere lost her employment because of organization scaling back. Rather than feeling crushed, she saw this as a chance to seek after another profession way.

Emily carved out opportunity to evaluate her abilities, interests, and market requests. She signed up for applicable courses, connected with experts in her ideal field, and adjusted her resume to feature adaptable abilities. Through her assurance and eagerness to adjust, Emily effectively changed into another vocation that lined up with her interests.

Migration

John and Lisa have been living in a clamoring city their entire lives. Notwithstanding, because of monetary requirements, they needed to migrate to a modest community. At first, they had an uneasy outlook on the change, abandoning commonality and their social encouraging group of people.

To adjust to this life change, they participate in local area exercises, join nearby clubs, and contact neighbors. Through their transparency and readiness to embrace the new climate, John and Lisa fabricate significant associations, find new open doors, and make a feeling of having a place in their new home.

Relationship change

Emma and Imprint have been in a drawn out relationship and choose to get hitched and move in together. As they combine their lives and schedules, they face difficulties in splitting the difference and changing in accordance with one another's propensities and inclinations. To adjust to this life change, they take part in transparent correspondence, effectively pay attention to one another's requirements, and track down clever fixes to keep up with concordance and backing in their relationship.

Instances of changes in the working environment

Working environment elements continually advance because of new jobs, group changes, or moving business techniques. Here are a few normal instances of adjusting to hierarchical changes:

Embracing new advancements

Alex, an undertaking chief, experienced an adjustment of hard working attitudes when his organization executed another venture the board programming. Instead of opposing the change, Alex decided to embrace it as a chance for proficient development. He effectively searched out preparing assets, went to online classes, and teamed up with associates who were at that point capable in the product.

Changing to remote work

Sarah, a showcasing proficient, wound up confronting a massive change when her organization progressed to remote work because of a worldwide pandemic. Rather than feeling overpowered, She immediately changed her workplace at home, made an organized daily practice, and investigated different computerized coordinated effort instruments to guarantee consistent correspondence with her group.

Adjusting to authoritative rebuilding

Karen, a senior leader, confronted a significant hierarchical rebuilding inside her organization. Rather than feeling demotivated or safe, she invited the change as a chance to reclassify her job and add to the organization's development. Karen looked for criticism from her bosses, proactively distinguished regions where she could offer some incentive, and adjusted her abilities to meet the developing requirements of the association.

Assisting messes around with learning versatility

Assisting youngsters with adjusting to changes is vital for their profound prosperity and development. Here are a few techniques to help kids in embracing new encounters:

Speak with care

This is imperative in aiding kids comprehend and adjust to change. The following are the steps to take to make it happen:

- Make sense of the impending change for your kid in an unmistakable and age-proper way.

- Urge them to pose inquiries about the change.

- Give consolation and underline that change is an ordinary piece of life.

Keep up with schedules and commonality

Making a feeling of commonality and routine can provide kids with a conviction that all is good during change. How it's done:

- In the event that conceivable, bring along natural items, like a most loved toy or cover, while moving to another climate. These natural things can give solace and a feeling of commonality.

- Lay out a predictable day to day daily schedule for your kid that gives design and solidness.

- Assist your kid with understanding the new normal related with the change.

Empower profound articulation

Cultivate close to home prosperity in your youngsters by empowering them to communicate their sentiments.

- Make a place of refuge for your kid to straightforwardly communicate their feelings and concerns.

- Urge your youngster to utilize age-proper apparatuses to communicate their feelings, like drawing, composing, or narrating.

- Show your kid solid survival techniques, like profound breathing activities, enjoying reprieves, or taking part in proactive tasks, to really deal with their feelings.
- Support associations

Work with an encouraging group of people and associations for youngsters during seasons of progress.

- Urge your youngster to assemble new kinships and associations in their new climate. Joining clubs, partaking in local area exercises, or organizing playdates can assist with working with this cycle.

- In the event that the change includes a school progress, contact educators or school guides for extra help.

Normal confusions about adjusting to change

Adjusting to change is an expertise that is turning out to be progressively significant in our speedy world. Nonetheless, there are a few confusions that frequently block people from embracing change successfully.

We should check out at a portion of the fantasies and put any misinformation to rest.

Adjusting to change implies shortcoming or give up

Adjusting to change is definitely not an indication of shortcoming or disappointment; as a matter of fact, it is a strength. It includes getting out of one's usual range of familiarity and embracing new open doors for development and self-awareness.

Adjusting to change implies undermining one's qualities and convictions

Adjusting to change doesn't be guaranteed to mean undermining your qualities and convictions. It's tied in with being adaptable in moving toward circumstances and tracking down ways of exploring new conditions while remaining consistent with your center standards.

Adjusting to change implies moving on to bigger and better things

Adjusting to change isn't tied in with disposing of the past. Our previous encounters, whether positive or negative, shape who we are today. They give significant illustrations, experiences, and abilities that can be applied in new circumstances. Adjusting to change expects us to draw upon our previous encounters and incorporate them into our current reality.

Adjusting to change is consistently awkward and upsetting.

While change can at times be awkward and unpleasant, it doesn't need to be a consistent state. Adjusting to change includes creating flexibility and learning powerful survival techniques to oversee pressure and distress.

Adjusting to change is just essential in significant life altering situations

Adjusting to change is significant in different parts of life, not just significant life altering situations. Change happens in day to day schedules, connections, work, and individual objectives. Embracing change and adjusting to new conditions assists people with taking full advantage of chances, keep up with importance, and lead satisfying lives.

Conquering difficulties with adjusting to change

Embracing change is generally difficult, and a few people might experience different difficulties en route. The following are a few impediments to adjusting to change and viable answers for beat them.

Anxiety toward the unexplored world

While confronting the obscure, dread and vulnerability can thwart our capacity to adjust to change. Conquering this challenge requires at least one of the accompanying:

Recognize your feelings of dread: Perceive and acknowledge that dread is a typical reaction to change.

Center around conceivable outcomes: Instead of harp on the negative parts of the obscure, shift your attitude towards the potential open doors that change can bring.

Make little strides: Separate the change into sensible undertakings or objectives. By moving forward, you can progressively construct certainty and diminish the apprehension about the unexplored world.

Protection from change

Protection from change is a typical obstacle throughout everyday life and vocation changes. This is the way to explore this:

- **Look for help:** Encircle yourself with an organization of companions, family, or coaches who can energize and direct you through the change cycle. Their points of view and encounters can assist you with acquiring new bits of knowledge and conquered opposition.

- **Rethink change as a decision:** Perceive that change is unavoidable and that embracing it is a cognizant decision. By reexamining change as a functioning choice as opposed to something constrained upon you, you can recover control and strengthening.

Absence of adaptability

Unbending assumptions and assumptions can ruin our capacity to actually explore new conditions. Here are ways of conquering this test:

- **Practice self-reflection:** Find opportunity to look at your convictions, presumptions, and assumptions. Is it safe to say that they are serving you well even with change? Be available to testing and changing your points of view to more readily line up with new real factors.

- **Develop flexibility:** Foster versatility by developing your profound fortitude and adapting abilities. Strong people can return from difficulties and adjust all the more effectively to change.

- **Embrace a learning mentality:** Move toward change with a readiness to learn and develop. Treat each new experience as a valuable chance to acquire new experiences, abilities, and information.

Conquering the past

Previous encounters and injuries can altogether affect our capacity to embrace change and jump all over new chances. Here are techniques to assist you with conquering this test:

- **Look for proficient assistance:** On the off chance that previous encounters are essentially influencing your capacity to adjust, think about looking for the direction of a specialist or guide. They can offer help and assist you with handling unsettled feelings.

- **Practice self-empathy:** Be caring and delicate with yourself as you explore change. Recognize that it's not unexpected to have psychological weight and allow yourself to mend and develop at your own speed.

- **Center around the present:** Rather than harping on previous encounters, center around the current second and the potential outcomes it holds. Practice care and establishing strategies to assist you with remaining fixed on the present time and place.

Quotes about adjusting to changes

When confronted with new conditions or changes, looking for motivation from the insight of others can be useful. Pause for a minute to consider these clever expressions and track down strength in embracing change.

- "Versatility isn't impersonation. It implies the force of obstruction and osmosis." - Mahatma Gandhi
- Versatility is the basic mystery of endurance." - Jessica Hagedorn

Last considerations

Versatility isn't just about endurance; it's tied in with embracing development and quickly taking advantage of chances. Make the following stride by rehearsing flexibility in your everyday existence. Embrace change and look for help when required.

Thriving in a Dynamic Workplace

In the cutting edge business scene, pioneers should develop workplaces that are helpful for organizations staying aware of the requests of the market. Notwithstanding, this quest for efficiency and advancement can some of the time come to the detriment of worker prosperity.

While it might appear to be a troublesome equilibrium to strike, it is feasible for pioneers to make dynamic working environments that likewise support representative prosperity. The following, are a few powerful methodologies pioneers can use to make a flourishing, high-performing workplace while likewise focusing on the all encompassing strength of their groups.

1. Search For Worth Adjusted Up-and-comers

The force of employing colleagues who are esteem adjusted can't be put into words. In the event that pioneers want a dynamic, speedy, high-energy climate, worry for worker prosperity ought to begin in the employing system. By searching for up-and-comers who likewise embrace change, are development disapproved and are propelled by a high speed culture, they can guarantee worker prosperity will remain closely connected with firm achievement.

2. Guarantee There Is Trust Among The Group

In the master administrations space, a powerful workplace and representative prosperity remain closely connected. Most staff today realize that change is unavoidable. What's not inescapable is the way associated they feel to their chiefs and the amount they trust those pioneers to direct them through the change. At the point when pioneers serious areas of strength for construct with staff before a problematic change happens, things go much better.

3. Have Transparent Group Correspondence

Pioneers should convey clear assumptions and characterize what greatness in real life resembles. With viable and open correspondence as an establishment, an association is situated to deal with change both inside and remotely because of market needs. To oversee representative prosperity, pioneers should realize what their workers esteem and guarantee there are open doors for their voices to be heard and perceived.

4. Show Your Group You Care About Them

Establish a mentally protected workplace to empower the group to be strong and adjust to change, while likewise empowering them to shout out when feelings of anxiety get too high so the pioneer can change as needs be. As a pioneer, I can't help and make changes in the event that I don't realize help is required. Make wellbeing via mindful. Guarantee there are an adequate number areas of strength for of, clearness, independence and value inside the group. They will respond via mindful also.

5. Guarantee Outright Lucidity On Work Assumptions

When assumptions are straightforward and settled upon, then, at that point, it means quite a bit to check in with workers to guarantee they have every one of the sensible assets they need, including the right help and care for their prosperity. This will assist them with measuring up to assumptions and manage change really.

6. Grasp How To Adjust 'Exertion And Simplicity'

Get to be aware and explore the pressures that emerge in adjusting "exertion and simplicity." Exertion incorporates commitment, drive and accomplishment — all fundamental to extraordinary results. However, a lot of exertion, and the groups break. Learn apparatuses and techniques that gain by the advantages of straightforwardness — the capacity to rest, reestablish and rejuvenate groups. Make brilliant courses of action and approaches that honor the existence cycle and advantages of both.

7. Share The Taking care of oneself Strategies That Work For You

Aircraft rules work — secure your own cover first. What has been working for you in attempting to deal with your prosperity? Sharing what works for you assists representatives with normalizing taking care of oneself discussions. One pioneer kept a normal health sign on his wall. As representatives saw his obligation to appearing for himself with the goal that he could appear for them, new discussions were ignited, prompting fun change.

8. Focus on Workers' Prosperity And Your Own

To establish a powerful workplace to stay up with transform, it is significant to focus on representatives' prosperity to construct strength and forestall burnout. Start to lead the pack by focusing on your own prosperity, and you will allow your representatives to follow. Make a move to remind representatives that their prosperity is basic to your organization's drawn out progress.

9. Make A Mentally Protected Work environment

A powerful climate is one where thoughts are continually created — and thoughts need space, time, opportunity and mental security. It accepts mental fortitude as a pioneer to abandon the order and-control worldview and embrace a trust-based worldview; yet without trust, there's no ease! Center around being completely clear, building exchanges and connections and empowering individuals to communicate what their identity is.

10. Show others how its done

Show others how its done by not just conversing with workers about their prosperity, yet additionally by having substantial arrangements that representatives can utilize. As their chief, be the trailblazer in utilizing them first. On the off chance that the is carrying out a care program, the pioneer ought to be the first to effectively utilize it to show its significance.

11. Much of the time Screen Representative Prosperity

How would you keep your finger on the beat? By genuinely taking a look at the beat. In a powerful climate, tracking down approaches to really and oftentimes screen worker prosperity and answer when changes are required is vital. Assuming your labor force is depleted or focused, that ideal dynamism won't appear economically. Models incorporate physical and mental prosperity checks and appraisals.

12. Advance Development, Development And Balance between fun and serious activities

A pioneer can establish a powerful workplace by cultivating open correspondence, empowering trial and error and development and giving open doors to representative development and improvement. Simultaneously, they can focus on representative prosperity by advancing balance between fun and serious activities, offering psychological wellness assets and esteeming and perceiving worker commitments.

13. Permit Your Group To Seek clarification on some pressing issues

Straightforwardness and trust are central components that will assist a pioneer with overseeing change. It begins with being purposeful about the thing is being conveyed and establishing a climate for the group to clarify pressing issues and gain understanding. Embracing a mentor chief mentality might be instrumental in guaranteeing your capacity to explore it well.

14. Establish A Climate Where Individuals Won't hesitate To Fizzle

Establish a climate where individuals will be imaginative and don't fear disappointment. Make a move to gain from the two triumphs and disappointments as a method for maintaining a flexible mindset. Join this with an unmistakable vision and needs that carry concentration to what is significant. Be adaptable about "how" individuals are conveying their work. Praise achievement and prize individuals' endeavors.

15. Assist Your Kin With staying balanced

Who said prosperity and a unique workplace are totally unrelated? Notwithstanding the negative and enduring impact on those influenced, worker burnout has a huge negative drag on efficiency and cost. Gallup reports $322 billion lost all around the world in turnover and lost efficiency because of representative burnout. To start with, assistance your kin to be at their best assuming that you believe your business should succeed.

CHAPTER 12:

Sustaining Excellence

Okay, how about we quit wasting time. Building a tip top profession isn't a run; it's a long distance race. Supporting greatness in this excursion requires a mix of system, versatility, and a tenacious quest for development. No puff, simply the genuine article.

1. Set Clear, Noteworthy Objectives: Characterize your objectives like you're giving bearings. Make them explicit, quantifiable, reachable, significant, and time-bound (Savvy). These are your North Star; they guide each move you make.

2. Construct Executioner Propensities: Achievement is certainly not a one-time thing; it's a progression of smart activities rehashed reliably. Foster propensities that line up with your objectives. Whether it's getting up at 5 AM, crushing out an exercise, or devoting time everyday to learning, propensities shape your direction.

3. Embrace Long lasting Learning: The work market is a wild wilderness, and the most effective way to explore it is by remaining sharp. Peruse, take courses, go to studios. The more you learn, the more you acquire, and not simply with regards to cash.

4. Network Like Your Profession Relies upon It (Since It Does): Your organization is your total assets. Try not to simply gather business cards; fabricate significant connections. Go to industry occasions, connect on LinkedIn, and recall, veritable associations beat 1,000 shallow contacts.

5. Ace Using time productively: Time is your most important resource. Figure out how to focus on undertakings, embrace the 5 AM way of life assuming it suits you, use efficiency apparatuses, and mercilessly cut out time-squandering exercises.

6. Handle Misfortunes Like an Ace: In your profession, you'll confront mishaps - dismissed recommendations, bombed projects, perhaps a formal notice. Try not to pout. Gain from it, change your procedure, and quickly return more grounded. Strength is your unmistakable advantage.

7. Look for Input, In any event, When It Stings: Useful analysis is your companion, not your foe. Effectively look for criticism, particularly when it's awkward. It's the quickest method for detecting your vulnerable sides and step up.

8. Balance Work and Life (Indeed, It's Conceivable): Wearing out won't make you world class. Figure out how to adjust work and life. Enjoy reprieves, invest energy with friends and family, and recall that a very much refreshed mind is a high-performing mind.

9. Remain Versatile in a Moving Scene: Businesses develop, innovations change, and pandemics occur. Remain versatile. Watch out for patterns, be available to novel thoughts, and be prepared to turn when required.

10. Improve and Remain Ahead: Don't simply follow the group; lead it. Improve in your field. Remain on the ball by expecting patterns and being the individual others look to for direction.

11. Put resources into Your Psychological and Actual Well-being: Your brain and body are your most significant resources. Work-out consistently, practice care, and guarantee you're in top condition to handle the difficulties that come your direction.

12. Develop a Positive Work Environment: Your environmental elements influence your presentation. Fabricate a positive workplace. Encircle yourself with spurred people who move and challenge you.

13. Construct an Individual Brand: In the time of web-based entertainment, your own image matters. Grandstand your ability, share your experiences, and let the world in on what makes you novel in your field.

14. Plan for the Long Term: Think long distance race, not run. Plan as long as possible. Your profession is an excursion, not an objective. Have a dream and adjust your arrangement depending on the situation.

15. Ponder and Refine: Regularly mirror your excursion. What worked? Actually what didn't? Change your methodology likewise. Constant improvement is the situation.

Building a tip top vocation is certainly not a mysterious society; it's a progression of purposeful activities. It's about reliably appearing, adjusting to change, and remaining consistent with your objectives. Thus, gear up, in light of the fact that supporting greatness isn't an undertaking; it's a lifestyle. Go smash it!

Keeping up with and Developing Your Tip top Vocation

OK, secure. Staying aware of and growing a top of the line occupation is surely not a walk around the recreation area, yet it's not exorbitantly convoluted on the other hand. We ought to hop straight into the channels with some feasible, human guidance.

1. Change or Get Abandoned: In the master wild, Darwin's standard applies - change or die. Ventures create, developments advance, and examples change. Stay legitimate. Keep on learning, embrace new devices, and don't be the individual adhering to outdated procedures.

2. Keep the Hankering Alive: Recollect that energy when you started? Keep it consuming. Stay hungry for progress. Absence of concern is the enemy of improvement. Set new challenges, seek after additional capacities, and keep that forceful blaze alive.

3. Putting together Keeps forever: Organizing is most certainly not a one-time event; it's a dependable trip. Keep on expanding your master circle. Go to gatherings, partner on LinkedIn, and get coffee with industry peers. Nobody can tell when an affiliation could open a doorway.

4. Foster Your Scope of abilities: Abilities are your money. Assess the market demands and foster your scope of capacities as necessary. Whether it's overwhelming another programming language or making drive capacities, they stay huge and significant.

5. Proceed Possibly risky courses of action: The top notch will not hold back to wager whenever the odds are good that on the side of themselves. Do whatever it takes not to be insane, but try to proceed painstakingly thought out strategies. Whether it's contributing to a troublesome endeavor or starting a subsequent work, risk much of the time prompts reward.

6. Be the Issue Solver: Try not to just perceive issues; address them. Transform into the primary resource who can fix things. It could mean bouncing into a disaster area, but being the issue solver is a trustworthy strategy for making yourself basic.

7. Embrace Organization Potential open doors: Administration isn't just about supervising people. It's connected to moving, coordinating, and driving results. Search for drive to open entryways, whether or not it suggests driving a little endeavor. It's the best method for working on your drive capacities.

8. Orchestrate Like a Master: Whether it's your remuneration, project courses of occasions, or a game plan with a client, become the best at conversation. Your ability to orchestrate impacts your benefit and your effect.

9. Remain Educated: Regardless of whether you're not in a tech-driven work, development impacts every industry. Stay instructed.

Understand emerging headways, how might affect your industry, and how you can utilize them.

10. Coach and Be Mentored: Mentorship is certainly not a single direction road. Find a coach who can direct you, and furthermore guide another person. A cooperative relationship encourages development on the two closures.

11. Brand Yourself Effectively: Your individual brand is your expert standing. Develop it. Utilize virtual entertainment decisively, exhibit your skill, and let individuals in on what you offer of real value.

12. Encourage a Solid Work-Life Integration: Notice I said mix, not balance. Actually, at times work requests more, and some of the time life takes the front seat. Find what works for you to keep up with your mental stability and succeed in your vocation.

13. Enhance Your Experience: Don't become a tired old act. Enhance your experience. On the off chance that you've spent your profession in one industry, investigate others. Alternate points of view and encounters make you an additional versatile and significant expert.

14. Fabricate a Heritage, In addition to a Career: Think past the following advancement or venture. What heritage would you like to leave? How would you like to be recalled? Building an inheritance mentality assists you with settling on choices that add to your drawn out influence.

15. Focus on Well-being: Your mental and actual wellbeing are non-debatable. Burnout doesn't make you tip top; it makes you depleted. Focus on taking care of oneself, get sufficient rest, and know when to make a stride back for your prosperity.

Keeping up with and growing a tip top vocation is certainly not an oddball task; it's a continuous responsibility. It's tied in with remaining lithe, hungry, and consistent with your qualities. An excursion requests versatility, flexibility, and a constant quest for greatness. Thus, go out there, break a couple of molds, and continue to develop. Your world class vocation is standing by.

Conclusion

As we stand at the crossroads of the past and the future, the tapestry of an elite career unfolds – woven with the threads of accomplishments, setbacks, growth, and relentless pursuit. The journey is uniquely yours, a narrative that continues to evolve with every choice and every moment of reflection.

Reflecting on the Elite Career Journey: A Personal Odyssey

In the hustle and bustle of the professional realm, pausing to reflect on the journey becomes an invaluable exercise. It's about figuring out the complex patterns that have influenced your career path, not about living in the past.

Remember those wins? The times when your efforts bore fruit, and success wasn't just a destination but a journey? Celebrate them. They are the milestones that mark your progress, the affirmations that you're on the right path.

And the setbacks? Those moments that felt like stumbling blocks? Don't shy away from them; dive in. Explore the lessons they carry. It's in understanding the nuances of failure that we find the seeds of future success.

Along this journey, growth is also a constant companion. Reflect on the transformation from the novice who entered the professional arena to the seasoned player you've become. Acknowledge the skills honed, the challenges conquered, and the resilience fostered.

The values that guide your decisions deserve a spot in the reflection room. In What matters most to you in your career? Whether it's innovation, collaboration, or a commitment to ethical practices, realigning with these values shapes the compass for your journey ahead.

Passion, the driving force behind every elite career, deserves a moment of introspection. What gets your heart racing, your mind buzzing, and your creativity flowing? Reconnecting with your passion rekindles the flame that propels you forward.

Work-life balance, that elusive dance between professional aspirations and personal well-being, requires scrutiny. Are you in sync with what truly matters outside the boardroom? Adjust as necessary because, in the grand scheme, a fulfilling career isn't achieved at the expense of a satisfying life.

Your network, a web of professional relationships, isn't just a LinkedIn list. It is a breathing, living thing that needs to be taken care of. Nurture genuine connections and release those that no longer contribute to your growth.

The network you cultivate is a reflection of your professional identity.

Mentorship, the invisible hand guiding your steps, holds profound significance. Reflect on the mentors who have left an indelible mark on your journey. If you haven't benefited from mentorship, consider the untapped potential it has to shape your career path.

Change, the only constant, is a recurring theme in any elite career. Reflect on how you've navigated change. Have you been agile, adapting to the shifting tides, or resistant, clinging to the familiar? Accepting change puts you in a leadership position as your career evolves.

Your personal brand, the essence of your professional identity, merits contemplation. How do you want to be perceived in the professional arena? Crafting and curating your personal brand is a deliberate exercise in steering your career narrative.

Setting new goals, the exhilarating leap into uncharted territories, is a vital part of reflection. What summits do you aspire to conquer? Whether it's a leadership role, a passion project, or a career pivot, articulating these goals propels you toward a purposeful future.

A Future of Possibilities: Painting Tomorrow's Canvas

Now, let's cast our gaze into the future – a future teeming with possibilities, waiting to be unraveled and explored. You hold the brush, and the canvas is empty.

In this future landscape, continuous learning emerges as the cornerstone. The rapid evolution of industries demands an insatiable appetite for knowledge. Embrace the idea that learning isn't a phase but a lifelong commitment. It's the bridge between your present and the cutting edge of tomorrow.

Technology, the double-edged sword shaping industries, positions itself as your ally. Remain tech-savvy so that you can actively participate in the technological narrative rather than just being a passive user. Recognize the ways in which new technologies can improve your abilities and your impact.

Dexterity and flexibility become your superpowers. In our current reality where change is the main steady, the people who can turn quickly and exquisitely will arise as pioneers. Develop the mentality that sees change not as an interruption but rather as a chance for development.

The ability to appreciate individuals on a profound level, frequently eclipsed by specialized ability, becomes the dominant focal point.

The human touch, the capacity to comprehend and deal with feelings - yours and others - turns into a key differentiator. It's not just about being great at what you do; it's tied in with being great with individuals.

A worldwide viewpoint, when a beneficial quality, turns into a need. The future expert rises above public limits in their work. Develop a comprehension of different societies, work together with global groups, and value the wealth of a globalized world.

Organizing, a lasting resource, rises above actual limits. In the advanced age, your organization reaches out past gathering corridors and espresso gatherings. Capitalize on web assets, partake in internet based networks, and lay out an overall expert brand.

Remote work, when an exemption, hardens its place as a key shift. It takes something beyond specialized capability to turn into a specialist at remote work; you likewise should have the option to convey really, balance your own and proficient lives, and flourish in a dispersed work environment.

An innovative mentality, recently connected with new companies, turns into an essential for all. Whether you're a business person or some portion of a huge enterprise, thinking imaginatively, proceeding with carefully weighed out courses of action, and embracing a feeling of responsibility become essential to your prosperity.

Supportability, in addition to a popular expression yet a business basic, becomes the dominant focal point. Ponder the effect of your work on the climate and society. What's to come has a place with the people who mesh manageability into the texture of their professions.

Information proficiency, when a specialty expertise, becomes universal. The capacity to decipher, investigate, and influence information for independent direction turns into a center capability. Whether you're in money, advertising, or medical services, information education is the cash of tomorrow.

Since they offer the human touch, delicate abilities are turning out to be progressively significant in a world that is turning out to be increasingly computerized.

Communication, collaboration, creativity, and critical thinking become the bedrock of your success, complementing your technical prowess.

Health and well-being, often neglected in the pursuit of success, claim their rightful place. The future professional understands that peak performance isn't sustainable without a foundation of physical and mental well-being. It's not just about climbing the ladder; it's about staying healthy while doing so.

Once seen as a threat, AI and human collaboration now have a mutually beneficial relationship. Understand how AI can enhance your work and collaborate effectively with these technologies. Collaboration between humans and AI becomes the rule rather than the exception.

Ethical leadership, a timeless virtue, becomes non-negotiable. In an era of transparency, ethical decisions aren't just commendable; they're expected. Aligning your professional choices with ethical principles is an investment in long-term success.

Purpose-driven careers, a rising trend, gain prominence. The future professional seeks more than a paycheck; they seek meaning in their work. Understand how your contributions align with a greater cause, whether it's social impact, environmental sustainability, or community development.

Progress's lifeblood, innovation, turns into a personal mandate. Don't just follow the

crowd; lead it. Innovate within your field, anticipate trends, and be the person.

Review page

Dear Reader,

Your spotlight second! 🎉 This page is where your considerations become the headliner. Disregard the customs, drop your genuine, unfiltered take on the book. Make a plunge, spill the tea, since this space blossoms with your energy!

Just wrapped up the book? Was it a rollercoaster ride, a quiet walk, or in the middle between? Hit us with your proud survey underneath! I should transform this space into a humming center of genuine discussion about vocations and life. Your words may very well be the mystery ingredient that persuades somebody to hop into this artistic experience. Overall, what are you holding your breath for? You have the stage to yourself!